The Family of The Retarded Child

By

JOHN N. AND NELLIE ENDERS CARVER

Syracuse University Division
of Special Education and
Rehabilitation and the
Center on Human Policy

SECOND IN A SERIES:
SEGREGATED SETTINGS AND
THE PROBLEM OF CHANGE

BURTON BLATT
SEYMOUR B. SARASON
HARRIETT D. BLANK
EDITORS

LIBRARY OF CONGRESS
CATALOGUE CARD NUMBER: 72-85384

First Edition 1972

Additional copies of this book may be ordered from:
SYRACUSE UNIVERSITY PRESS
Box 8, University Station
Syracuse, New York 13210

Manufactured in the United States of America

Table of Contents

The Center on Human Policy
is currently supported by
Grants No. 56-P-71003-2-01 and
55-P-10158-2-01 from the
Department of Health, Education and Welfare,
Social and Rehabilitation Service

Editors' Foreword

Almost two decades ago, the late John Carver began a dissertation that, eventually, became an academic classic, in spite of the fact that it is essentially unavailable, consequently unread, and therefore without the prominence it deserves. At the time of his work on *Reactions of Parents of Severely Retarded Children at a State Training School,* Yale University, 1956, promises were made to families and to agencies that strenuous measures would be taken, both to guarantee the anonymity of each family participating and to restrict circulation on the study within a very limited, carefully screened, group of scholars. It was hoped that John and Nellie Carver, his wife and collaborator throughout this research, eventually would write a book for general dissemination, one that would contain the essential substance and depth of the original dissertation. It was hoped that, with the passage of time and the maturation of ideas, a book would be written that violated no confidence yet shared and illuminated the activities, values, and burdens of a special sample of families that, quite possibly, John Carver was the first to study seriously in this age.

The years passed while Carver's research remained hidden from public scrutiny. However, during that time, this unique team labored to prepare the manuscript that became *The Family of the Retarded Child.*

There may be some who will question the capability of a state school to provide any valuable human service and, therefore syllogistically, question the value of this book. Those that think this way may miss the essence of the Carvers' contribution, the richness of their data and the painful singular honesty of these remarkable authors.

Hemingway may have said it best, although so did others before and after; the necessary gift the writer must preserve is an honesty, a belief that one's work rings true. Truth has its own beauty and value and purity. To complete this work, the Carvers needed endless and courageous honesty. For that reason—irrespective of our differences, our ideologies, our "facts"—this creation stands above the rest.

B. B.
S. B. S.
H. D. B

Names in this book have been changed to protect
the identity of the children and their families,
the doctors and private nursing homes and hospitals.

Preface

This book really had its beginning with the responses we received to this letter, which we wrote our old friends and relatives:

Dear Friend:

For a long while we had been concerned over the irregular pattern of Davey's mental development, although his rugged health, sweet disposition, and generally alert and helpful spirit allayed our fears for a time.

Last fall (at age four), however, we took him for testing to the Yale Child Study Center, where they found his trouble to be organic—probably congenital—and of a severity that will prevent him from ever coping with a normal social and school environment. We were urged to seek an early admission for him to the state training school at Southbury, before the widening gap between him and other children of his chronological age should become a source of distress to him and to us. They were surprised at the complete absence of the emotional disturbance that generally accompanies such a condition; on this basis they ventured to predict that his adjustment to the school would not be too difficult. The X-ray doctors at the Yale Medical School subsequently confirmed this diagnosis that David is a brain-damaged child in finding evidence of atrophy of the left cerebral hemisphere.

We have just been advised that there is a place now for David at Southbury Training School; the formalities of entrance being completed, we are taking him up there this week. These next few months will be the hardest for all three of us, but after Davey is adjusted somewhat we'll be able to go regularly to see him, and later on have him home for vacations. Southbury Training School is outstanding; it will provide him with an environment in which he can preserve his feeling of security and a teaching program that will help him learn to do everything that he is potentially able to accomplish. They have a very fine medical and educational staff.

The school is in a beautiful location in the hill-and-valley section of the state less than an hour's drive from New Haven. The small cottages in which the children live are ranged over a hillside campus above the playing fields and school buildings. We are very fortunate since we three must have this problem, that Connecticut provides such a place for children like David.

Our immediate plans include participating in the foster care program of the New Haven Children's Center; we expect to care for two children from there in our home this fall. We shall both get back to studying too. Nell has been accepted in the master's program jointly sponsored by Yale and the State Board of Education and will probably commence courses this fall. I'll be getting back to work on my dissertation.

We have had the greatest of help this past year with David from our friends here in the college community and at the University. Understandably, we've been reluctant to write our old friends about this deep trouble. We believe, though, now that we have started to work things out, that you should hear from us about it. This letter seems to be the best means.

NELL AND JOHN CARVER
August, 1953

The specific suggestion that we do a study of parents of severely retarded children came first from the late Dr. Clement C. Fry, long-time director of the Mental Health section of Yale's Department of University Health; but there was also the interest this letter evoked from other friends to whom we sent it—and *their* friends to whom they showed it. Their replies always showed a wish to understand, and sometimes even a need to share with us a comparable family problem. The way they responded to what we wrote made us wonder whether this experience had given us some special insight beyond our own predicament. It encouraged us to believe that we could make a substantive contribution to a clearer understanding of the impact of retardation, for all parents and friends of retarded children—personal and professional. What success we have had in this was abetted by the astute and thoughtful counsel of the late Ernest N. Roselle, superintendent of Southbury Training School, and members of his staff, in particular Dr. E. Louise Porter, and our advisors in the Yale Graduate School: Professors J. Warren Tilton, James Davie, and Seymour Sarason. In retrospect, doing the study was of immeasurable help toward our own adjustment. It made us realize that our problem with Davey was not unique but part of a universal problem—the tragedy of broken relationships.

Introduction

This book is about a group of parents, unique only in that they are parents of severely retarded children. Each set of parents was living together, maintaining a home for a family that was intact (except that one child had been placed in a state training school after an unsuccessful attempt to rear and care for him at home).

The subject of study, originally a doctoral study at Yale, was the parents' response to having a severely retarded child: what aspects of their family behavior had been affected, how severe these effects were, what specific experiences had been crucial for them—and how they felt about these experiences.

Our data were derived from an interview with parents of such children, based on a schedule of 76 questions which dealt with these parents' social relationships and behavior in three areas—within the immediate family; with close friends and relatives; and with neighbors, acquaintances, and the community. Social relationships and behavior we construed to mean all the bonds that tie the family together and the processes through which the family functions.

There are important things which all families do; the way the family with a severely retarded child does these things was our concern. Had their lives been permanently changed during their working out of the problem? Were they still operating outside the culture? These normal parents with a peculiar problem discussed with the authors the things they thought were important and shed some light on these questions.

The families in the study group lived in an industrial and suburban residence community. They comprised a cross section of socioeconomic status. There were homes in settings approaching gracious country living as well as some in congested poor neighborhoods. There were no families living on farms.

The behavior of this set of parents was influenced by some unique circumstances. Their community possessed excellent medical and psychological facilities for treating mentally retarded and physically handicapped children. The parents generally used these facilities, trusted the professionals who staffed them, and tried to follow their recommendations. Also, this community was served by an exceptionally fine state training school that really stressed the education and training of patients.

This school had prestige and acceptance in the community. With some allowance for these circumstances, it would seem quite reasonable to generalize about the behavior of parents of severely retarded children anywhere from the reactions of these families.

Because the severely retarded at any age must continue to be dependent persons, any provision for their welfare needs to take account of their families, the ones upon whom they have been dependent. Often it is through the families of these children that something constructive can be done. It may not be possible to do much directly to improve the *child's* status. Recently there has been a great effort to help severely retarded children, and their parents. But how to help them effectively? Some direction may be found by studying what these families have actually experienced in their day-to-day living. The measures, tactics, and techniques which some of the more resourceful of the parents evolved may help others who are confronted with the same problem.

The need for such help for these families is great. Thus far, the response has been generally superficial. Most of the studies of the behavior of such families have come out of interview contacts with them, perhaps just with the mother, in a clinic environment at a time of crisis. To generalize about parents' attitudes or behavior patterns by observing their conduct while they are being told for the first time that their child must be committed to a state institution seems questionable.

In a leisurely, informal home interview the parents in our study looked back on three successive periods in their lives: the time when they were learning that their child was severely retarded and coping with him at home, the time of having this child placed at the state training school at Southbury, and a brief segment of time subsequent, when they might have attained some perspective on their child's problem.

The severely retarded child is one whose functioning in life is minimal. He may not be totally dependent, but he cannot be independent ever. He may be trainable in simple behaviors, but he can never be educated. Occasionally, he may have the potential for sound physical health and a stable emotional constitution; on the other hand, he may be very severely handicapped, lacking even these possible assets.

In designing our study we decided on certain criteria for choosing the severely retarded children and their families: The child must have been classified as severely retarded (middle- or low-grade in the terminology the training school then employed). He must have been admitted no more than six years nor less than six months previously (since January 1950). He must have been a child (under age 20) at admission. His parents must have been maintaining a home together and living in greater New Haven.

There were 37 of these families (including ourselves); 30 of them were interviewed, and 30 case studies were prepared, 3 of which are included in Section II of this book. These 3 case studies or family profiles were chosen to cover a variety of family characteristics and a range of problems with the severely retarded child. What is common to them all is the courageous family effort to fit this handicapped child into the home and ultimately, failing in that, to adjust to placing him at the state training school.

If the reader desires, he may sample these profiles before reading the text of Section I. We would suggest, however, that everyone read over the sample interview at the end of this introduction to get an idea of the questions asked of the parents and the type of responses given.

The chapters in Section I are based chiefly on data, the product of the interview schedule. Chapters 1 through 5 derive from the first part of the interview—*At Time of Discovery;* Chapters 6 and 7 are based on the second part—*Going Away to the Training School.* The data for Chapter 8 derive from the third part—*Subsequent Experiences,* and our own observations of parents at Southbury since the interviews.

Chapter 1, "The Impact of Discovery," describes the process of discovery of their child's severe mental retardation and the impact on these parents: how they found out (and when) and how they reacted to the knowledge. The question of cause is touched on briefly.

Chapter 2, "The Severely Retarded Child," describes these severely retarded children and categorizes them in terms of the clinical types and the care problems they presented. The label "severely retarded" proved to be so broad as to include a wide range of symptoms and causes, disabilities and deficiencies. The inability to function adequately at home, even with strong support from their parents, was the common characteristic.

This chapter also recounts graphically in the parents' words how the child's condition or behavior affected the functioning of the family, and how he acted to assert his claim to family membership. The ways in which a severely retarded child related to his family for affection and attention influenced the picture his parents had of him, and the hopes they shared for his progress at home.

Chapter 3, "The Family Problem of the Retarded Child," focuses on the life of the nuclear family as modified by the severely retarded child's presence in the home. It describes how the parents behaved toward the child and toward each other in the context of this problem, and tells of the effects of this interaction on the husband and wife. It notes how family fertility was affected and how the everyday living patterns of the family were changed.

This chapter also considers the other children in the family: how the parents involved them, how these normal siblings behaved toward the retarded one, and how they seemed to be affected—at home and out in the community.

Chapter 4, "Family Relationships—Interaction with Others," covers the nuclear family's important relationships beyond the home but bearing upon it. It first tells how some parents availed themselves of continuing professional help in coping with the problem. It tells how family finances were affected—and the father's job. The chapter then describes how the family communicated with the neighbors in the light of this problem and how they interacted with intimate friends and close relatives.

Chapter 5, "Family Activity—Community and Associations," focuses on family activity outside the home. It takes note of the changes in social life and recreation patterns. It notes how the parents managed their impersonal contacts for their retarded child out in the wider community. It mentions their ties with the local Association for Retarded Children. The chapter describes the family stance toward church and other organizations, their religious participation and the part they took in civic and community affairs.

Chapter 6, "Waiting for a Place at Southbury," recounts the story of the families reluctantly moving toward the commitment of their severely retarded child. It tells of their gradual realization that they could not keep him home indefinitely and of their struggle to bring themselves to make an application to the training school. It assesses the slender hopes still remaining to them for their child.

This chapter also describes the parents' ambivalent feelings and the aggravated problems that arose during this long waiting period. It tells of further changes at home as they made preparations for the child's departure.

Chapter 7, "And Finally, Commitment of the Severely Retarded Child," tells of the events and feelings of commitment day itself, the immediate and later reactions of the families, and the response of the severely retarded child, through their first visits to him at the training school.

Chapter 8, "Readjustments and New Roles," traces the slow adjustment of the child to his life at the training school and the readjustment of the family at home to his absence. It closes by describing how child and family evolve a new set of role relationships with the help of the training school that bring some satisfactions to most—and relief to all.

Interview Schedule*

Face Sheet

Siblings	Age	Education
Brother: Timmy	*three years*	
Retarded girl: Margaret	*six years*	*At Southbury one year*

Others living in the household?
No

Religion
Roman Catholic

Father's job
Skilled technician

Father's Education
High school plus technical training in armed services

Does Mother work?
No

Mother's education
High school plus vocational training

* The sample schedule includes the response from one of the families participating in the study. The questions are all stated as though the retarded child was a male but at the time of the interview they were rephrased to fit the sex of the child. Often, the name of the child was also used in the questions.

Part I

At Time of Discovery

[The first three questions were answered together.]

1. How old was your child when you found out he was retarded?

2. How did you find out about it?

3. Who told you?

HUSBAND: At six months we noticed she was getting seizures.

WIFE: At six months we noticed something was wrong, not that she was retarded.

HUSBAND: Our own doctor had recommended we go to Dr. DeLeito. When she was about a year old Dr. DeLeito made an appointment for us to go to New Haven Hospital for an electroencephalogram. In two weeks we got a diagnosis of epilepsy from DeLeito, who prescribed triadon and phenobarbitol.

WIFE: The triadon slowed her down. It made her sluggish; she'd sleep all the time.

HUSBAND: That kid never smiled for two years.

WIFE: I was the one who wanted to stop going to Dr. DeLeito. Dr. DeLeito said, "There's nothing else I can do for her; maybe you'd better take her to the clinic." When she was about a year and a half we stopped going to Dr. DeLeito and went to the New Haven Hospital clinic where Dr. Samsel comes. Dr. Samsel took her off the triadon and gave her dilantin. He tried to control her seizures by varying the prescription of phenobarbitol.

HUSBAND: These jerks—we saw her do it a couple of times, but we weren't concerned for a couple of months.

WIFE: The grandmothers reassured us.

I think Dr. Samsel knew as soon as he saw her—her movements, what she did. He said, "Her mind is as a six months baby." That was when she was one and a half. He didn't know whether the spells or the medicine slowed her down. Time would tell. Nor did he tell us just whether the epilepsy was causing the retardation to be worse. He came right out and told us. I did not know whether I liked it or not. Every month I took her back to the clinic on a Wednesday when he would be there. He could not pinpoint just what it was. He would tell the interns: "Now watch this as she walks. There isn't a name for her. Her coordination, her mode of walking."

HUSBAND: At one and a half years he tried to explain retardation a little to us. He said, "She may have to have special training." But we didn't think he meant Southbury. I had been by it; it was just a pretty place on the side of a hill.

WIFE: I really hated to take her to the clinic; wait, sit and sit. They knew you were with a child you couldn't please. Dr. Samsel always wanted to see her in a spell at the clinic, but she never had one when he saw her there.

He'll come right out and tell you. One time when she was about two years old, he said, "There's no doubt about it; she'll have to be put away." Then he turned and went out. There was another woman doctor there.

HUSBAND: You had asked, "What are we going to do?" He said, "You'll have to put her in an institution." And he walked out.

WIFE: I think that's when we both realized.

HUSBAND: He had said earlier, "Put her application in. When the time comes for her to be admitted, you can refuse if you want to."

WIFE: But I wouldn't listen then.

We have liked Dr. Samsel. Anything he said was right. She will not sleep nights. I told him the worst I had with her was her not sleeping nights. He told me to put this nylon netting over her crib. I wouldn't do that.

HUSBAND: She'd work herself into a frenzy if we tried to hold her down.

WIFE: I couldn't tie her to the bed or lock her up at home and I told him so. He had told me to tie her in bed then. He said, "What do you think they will do at school?" This was after we had sent the application in. Then I began to think I didn't want to send her to school.

HUSBAND: When he said, "She can never have a normal life," that is when I felt bad.

4. Have you any idea what caused your child to be retarded?

WIFE: No, we have no idea. Although she did fall from the crib at six months. I carried her wonderful, and as far as her delivery, I never had any trouble.

5. How much did you know about retardation back at that time? Where had you learned it?

WIFE: I knew very little. Mostly in school I had heard about it, and then when we were kids there was a school.

HUSBAND: The "dumbbell school" over on Atwater Street. Kids can be cruel.

WIFE: I knew nothing about epilepsy.

HUSBAND: I didn't know much. I knew there was genius at one end and retarded at the other. There were epileptics at school, but I knew nothing about it.

WIFE: They used to call Margaret "Monkey." One time she was hidden from me by the shade, standing on the upper sash of the window. My little nephew came in crying. The kids outside had seen her and called her "Monkey."

6. Did you have any strong suspicions that something was wrong with your child long before this?

HUSBAND: At six months we noticed she was getting seizures.
[See Question 1.]

7. When you first found out that your child was retarded:
(a) How did you feel about it?
(b) How did your husband feel?

WIFE: I don't think there are any words. It hit me pretty hard. He did give us a warning. But the way he talked I felt that as she grew older, she'd catch up. But a little later when he came out and said there wasn't any help, I couldn't take that.

HUSBAND: That's a hard question.

WIFE: Yes, it is. The way he talked . . .

HUSBAND: He told us she would never lead a normal life. We thought perhaps a special school. We felt she'd progress but only a little slower than other kids.

WIFE: When he came out and said . . . He gave us no hopes. I think that's when we both realized.

8. What aspects of your child's trouble bothered you most back then? Was it something he used to do?

[In our preliminary conversation the husband realized we had some understanding of the hyperactive child. We described some of the things our child did. Everyone they had met at Parents' group meetings had "mongoloid children who could go to school and stay at home, not Southbury."]

HUSBAND: Did your child used to perch up on top of the refrigerator? Margaret did! She would get herself wrapped into the openings of the kitchen chair back, sit on the top and teeter back and forth with perfect balance. She rarely fell. She'd get up and stand on the edge of the sink, and reach up to turn on the light. [See also I, 12 and II, 4 for other hyperactive behavior. See I, 10 for her perseveration.]

WIFE: At two, she did not cause too much trouble. The only thing was that when she would get her spells, everyone would look, and she had a lot of them.

HUSBAND: She was a cute baby, very pretty, curly hair. The medicine spoiled her hair. No one knew there was anything wrong with her. [Here the father showed Margaret's picture.]

9. Was anything else going on in the family at that same time that made things even more difficult for you?

HUSBAND: *(turning to his wife)* Your father had quite a few heart attacks and shocks. You couldn't go to the hospital to see him because of Margaret. I remember you felt bad because you couldn't go with him.

10. Did you feel for a while that your child's trouble was somehow your fault?

WIFE: No

HUSBAND: I don't think so. The doctor said it could have been something in pregnancy. He seemed to think with Margaret it might have happened whatever you did. We're still trying to find out.

WIFE: I think the medicine slowed her down. At six months she was saying, "Dada," but now she'd go with anyone though.

HUSBAND: There's still recognition, I think; you can see that glint in her eye. She has a memory. She hadn't been home for six months. When I brought her home I drove past our corner, thinking I would take her for a minute to my mother. She yelled and screamed and jumped up and down in the car. I had to go around the corner and right back to our house. You can't console her. She gets one thing on her mind and that's it. One day my mother was taking care of her. She kept getting the toaster out and my mother kept putting it back, all day. Finally my wife's sister came in and my mother asked her about it. My wife's sister said, "Maybe she wants some toast." That was it! My mother spent the rest of the afternoon making toast and Margaret eating it! Once she put her elbow through the window—glass all over the place and jagged pieces still in the frame, but never a scratch on Margaret.

11. With whom did you discuss your child's problem back at that time?
(a) Doctor? *(c) Teacher?*
(b) Social worker? *(d) Someone else?*

HUSBAND: Just the family.

WIFE: We went to see Mr. Rothberg at the Children's Guidance Center. He again told us Southbury. She wasn't trainable. We gave him permission to go to New Haven Hospital to see her records. We wanted him to tell us about it in his own words.

HUSBAND: He told us a lot and yet he told us nothing.

12. Did you find it comfortable for you to talk with neighbors and friends about your child's being retarded?

WIFE: I did, but I think my husband found it harder.

[Silence from the husband, then] HUSBAND: Just the fellows I was associated with in the lab. But to me it seemed some of the things she did would mean nothing to them. They wouldn't get what I was trying to say. People like you know what I'm talking about. People in general don't know.

WIFE: He used to call me on the phone and sometimes I would say, "Wait a minute while I get Margaret off the refrigerator." Anyone listening in on the line would think . . .

HUSBAND: We had a friend, a cop and his wife, in for the evening. We were taking turns trying to settle Margaret down to sleep, and having a real hard time of it. Finally his wife said, "What's the matter with you two? The trouble is you two are too nervous." My wife said to her, "Jennie, you go in there and take over. You try to put her to sleep." After a while she came out of that room; she looked as though she had been in a jungle. She said, "Holy Mackerel!"

WIFE: I'm glad she did it.

HUSBAND: They never came much after that!

If at work I'd say, "My daughter stayed up all night," they would say, "Why did you let her?"

People would say, "Come and see us. Bring Margaret. She's no trouble." But that was because we never took our eyes off her for an instant. Once we took her on a family outing to Indian Wells. She had to be watched every minute. We put her between us at the picnic table and held her wrists to keep her at the table. And we'd take turns eating. I wish I had a dime for every time I put her shoes and socks back on. We had our eye on her every minute. The next week my mother asked us again. I said, "Mom, we don't *want* to go on the picnic; you know Margaret." And she said, "Why, that kid was a *doll* last week."

13. Did anyone give you advice on managing your child back at that time?

(a) Who were these people who were giving you advice?
(b) What was their advice?
(c) How did you feel about it?
(d) What did you do?
(e) Anybody else?
(f) Any other instance of advice?

WIFE: There was a lot of this from both our families: "Try to make her tired." [What would you do?] "Take her for walks." I could never take her for walks because if she spotted a car that looked like her father's she'd holler and scream. "A regular time for bed," they'd suggest.

HUSBAND: We had plenty of advice but nobody to help.

14. How did you as a family try to work things out after this trouble came?

(a) Did you seek professional help?
(b) Did you change family routine?

HUSBAND: We had no routine, any more. There were plenty of times when we never knew whether we would finish a meal. We ate when we got a chance to. Plenty of times when we were ready to sit down to a meal and she would disrupt a meal. Dr. Samsel, when we told him about this problem, said, "You forget she's a child, too."

WIFE: I did my work as I could during the day with her.

HUSBAND: Rainy days were terrible.

WIFE: Rainy days I would not do a thing except rock her and play that one record: "Don't Let the Stars Get in Your Eyes" with Perry Como.

I had some friends drop in. It had been six months since they visited. I had the same dungarees on and the same record was playing!

HUSBAND: You'd try to sit in one room with her. That same record—she'd go to sleep. You'd try to turn it off, you'd think a bomb had hit! She'd wake up instantly and want it back on. I fixed up the phonograph so that it would play over and over for her.

WIFE: I was going to write Perry Como about it.

HUSBAND: I used to come home some nights, take a look at my wife, and wonder if I should turn around and go back. [At such times he would bundle Margaret up and take her out in the car all evening.]

Take her out all evening until ten or eleven o'clock and she'd still be awake half of the night.

I'll bet my wife was in this house for two weeks straight without going out.

My wife used to say, "What's going through that kid's mind?"

WIFE: She'd whine for something, and we'd think, if we could only find out what to do to amuse her.

HUSBAND: The Mennen's Baby Powder can! She loved that, empty. We emptied more of those cans for her. She'd go up in my brother's bathroom and get a full one down and we'd have to empty it out and give it to her! Time after time! Once I was driving with her and she dropped the can of Mennen's at the intersection of Grove and Church. I drove quickly around the block, stopped the car in the middle of the street and dashed out into traffic to get it. It wasn't crushed!

WIFE: She was sly. She'd sneak up for something and then when she got it she would scoot into the other room. She liked to hum through stiff paper. She used to like big magazines.

HUSBAND: My wife used to have to sneak out after the Collier's magazine, tuck it under her skirts, and run into the bathroom with it and hide it under the bathtub before Margaret would see it. Or I'd never get to read it.

This house was stripped to the essentials, a stove and refrigerator, and she'd get up on top of both of them. Did your boy ever get into a gallon of Glo-Coat? Margaret did. She'd pull the doilies off the table and the curtains down. She spilled a bottle of Joy. Have you ever tried to clean up a bottle of Joy? If you put any water on it to clean it up, you're licked!

WIFE: We had a lot of New Year's Eve parties. She loved it. That was because everyone left her alone and she had free rein. Then with everybody feeling good, they would go home, and we would be up the rest of the night entertaining her.

15. Who took care of your child while he was still at home?
- *(a) Was she the only one?*
- *(b) Who else helped?*
- *(c) After you found out that your child was retarded, did someone else help?*

[The wife mostly. The husband would come home from work to help. When she was quite young, the husband's brother's wife took care of her for about four months. She'd take her for a whole day.]

WIFE: She was like a normal child then. And just when I went to the hospital for the baby, she took Margaret for two weeks. She was wonderful, she still is.

Then my kid sister would come in and take care of her for two hours between the time when I went to work and when my husband came home. This was for a period of over a year, up until Southbury. My sister did a wonderful job with her. She was only thirteen years old.

HUSBAND: She would change her; nights when I'd take Margaret to ride, she would come along. Those were the only two cases of help, though. I still do not think the family understands.

16. What did you think should be done for your child—what steps did you think should be taken?

(a) What did your husband think should be done?

(b) Was there any part of it where you differed?

(c) Any other part?

HUSBAND: We thought we could handle her.

WIFE: I did too.

HUSBAND: I asked Dr. Samsel, "Do you think they could do anything for her at Southbury that we couldn't?" He answered that the mother's care was best. At that early time all we thought was to keep her home. We thought if we spent enough time she would learn. We did not know about the hyperactivity, then. We've never been sorry we put her up there in Southbury. Without any shame, her fingernails—we have never seen her so clean. Those housegirls will just brush her hair by the hour. At home we could never get the snarls out of it.

[Differed?] No.

WIFE: Yes, he was trying to talk me into having her at Southbury, and I wouldn't hear of it, when she was three.

HUSBAND: I thought handling so many of them, Dr. Samsel should know.

WIFE: We put her application in when she was three and a half or four. She went when she was five. I think deep inside I knew he was right. I just hadn't come to it. I was not willing yet to admit that it had to be.

HUSBAND: Dr. Samsel gave me the talk: I was making it worse for Margaret. Up there she could have more fun and be with her own kind. And then seeing the school helped a little.

17. How did you feel about having more children after you discovered that your child was retarded? Did you try to get any professional advice about it?

WIFE: *(hesitation)* Well, it took me a long time to have one. I was afraid. You hear things, you know. My doctor said to go ahead, it wouldn't happen again—one in a million. We put her name on the emergency list—I thought I wouldn't feel so bad if I had a baby. He was just starting to walk when she went to Southbury.

HUSBAND: I guess so. I was scared. There was no guarantee.

WIFE: Dr. Samsel told me I should have another, that I should have gone right ahead and had another right after I found out about Margaret.

18. What did having your child do to your other children? How did it effect them?

(a) Did they accept more responsibility?
(b) Did they get unruly?
(c) Did they imitate the retarded child?

WIFE: He grew up faster.

HUSBAND: He had to take care of himself. We used to yell at him a little more than we should have, and jumped on him. We were on pins and needles.

WIFE: He wasn't babied as much. When he cried, he'd have his bottle.

HUSBAND: A lot of times just to console her, if there was an argument between them we would decide in her favor, give her the toy he had. He'd always have to wait until she put a toy down. Then we'd say to him, "She's dropped it. Go get it." But then she'd want it back again when she saw he had it.

WIFE: Being the first child it is the hardest. Everybody looks forward to their first child. There's more help from the older children if the retarded child is younger.

HUSBAND: Maybe in training and the bottle it was longer.

WIFE: Before she went it wasn't much use trying to toilet train him. It didn't take long to train him after she went up to Southbury. [They admitted to overtending him now.]

19. What was the attitude of your other children toward your child when he was still at home?

(a) How did they act toward him?
(b) How did they feel about him?

WIFE: I don't think he realized when Margaret was home that there was anything wrong. He was a year and a half when she went. It's only now that he has noticed and realizes that she is sick: "Margaret is just like Grandpa." My father recently had a stroke and cannot talk either. He is affectionate with her, he wants to hug and kiss her. She doesn't give him a chance to. He knows, at less than three years old, that she is his sister and he relates to her strongly. He said, "Why doesn't she talk?" He cried when we took her back to Southbury. She didn't bother him at all when she was at home, unless he had a toy that she wanted. She used to pick him up when he would climb up and stand by the window of the kitchen door, and dump him on the floor so that she could stand there.

20. In your opinion, what was the attitude of the neighbors and their children toward your child?
- *(a) How did they treat him?*
- *(b) How did they feel about him?*
- *(c) Was there anything else that happened with the neighbors or their children that you especially remember?*
- *(d) Looking back to this time of finding out, was there anything you recall doing that helped your neighbors and friends to treat your child with more understanding?*
- *(e) Was there anything you recall doing that caused misunderstanding with your neighbors and/or friends?*

WIFE: A lot of them knew there was something wrong with her.

HUSBAND: Because they would never see her out.

WIFE: There were a few of the kids who would have liked to take her for a walk, but I couldn't let them. They couldn't hold her and she could get out of the carriage. And she would have gotten into the street. I'd let her go out in the yard and tell them they could watch her so as not to hurt their feelings. I never got out enough to meet my neighbors.

HUSBAND: We explained it to the family—what it was, things like that. But I don't think the families even now understand what this means to us. They go by the school. Why don't they stop in? My wife says, "Well, it's easier if they don't."

WIFE: We tried it just once or twice letting her out in the fenced-in yard but she would holler so.

HUSBAND: A priest whose car I was working on across the street heard her yelling in the yard. He said, "What's wrong with the little girl?" I told him about her. He offered to help get her into Southbury.

The neighbors ignored it. They knew but they never bothered. We never said anything so they didn't to us. For all we know, they may say, "Remember the little kid on the corner that they would never let out."

WIFE: She loves water, the little wading pool in the back yard, but then she would sit on the edge of it and let the water out. The other kids would get mad, so I stopped taking her over there. I was fortunate I lived in my mother's house. She would bang and scream all day long.

They wouldn't put up with that anywhere else. The man downstairs in the store was very nice. He said he knows someone in Southbury.

HUSBAND: He said to me not long ago: "You know I miss that record your wife liked so much—"Don't Let the Stars Get in Your Eyes."

21. How about your close relatives—what was their attitude toward your child (grandparents, aunts, and uncles of the retarded child)?

(a) How did they treat him?

(b) How did they feel toward him (as a person)?

(c) Was there anything else that happened with your close relatives that you especially remember?

HUSBAND: Any home we went into they'd say, "Let her go."

WIFE: I was wondering if we really let her go, if she did break everything on them, I wonder what they'd say.

HUSBAND: We were tempted to take her to someone's house and when they said, "Let her go," to really let her go. Oh Baby! she would really . . .

People see her running madly up there at Southbury across the grounds and they think nothing of it. She could feel the atmosphere, the attitude of people. Mrs. Smith was so good to her. We were at their camp. Mrs. Smith is a good friend of Mr. Roselle.

22. These same close relatives—how much help did you get from them at that time?

(a) Moral support?

(b) Physical assistance?

(c) Did some of them make your handling of your child's trouble more difficult or criticize your management of the child?

WIFE: Well, they all helped. I think everybody would help if we asked them.

HUSBAND: None of them really offered, and there were a lot of opportunities.

On these family outings they'd say, "Why, she's just a little doll. You couldn't ask for a sweeter kid. She runs around like the other kids." But we'd sit on either side of her and hold her wrists to make her stay at the table and eat. We finally took her out and put her in the car. We let her tear the car apart inside and we sat on the running board.

WIFE: We used to love to take Margaret to parks.

HUSBAND: Let her run from one of us to the other. When she runs, she laughs. We love to see her run.

WIFE: Once your sister-in-law took Margaret—that same sister-in-law. She was the only one that knew Margaret. Anybody else we had to tell them too much. We went down to see your brother in North Carolina when he was in service.

HUSBAND: They were the kind who would let her do what she wanted to. "Let her go," they said; and she went it! Once she got my brother's pipe. I tried to take it away from her. He said, "Look, would you leave the kid alone?" She broke the pipe and he said to me, "So you're worried. Have you got to pay for it?"

23. Did finding out that your child was retarded make any difference in your activities and companionship with other people? Did it make any change in your life?

- *(a) Did it make any change in your interest and activity in club doings and neighborhood affairs?*
- *(b) Did it affect your other recreation?*
- *(c) Did it have any effect on your husband at his work?*
- *(d) Did it make any change in your going to church?*
  - *(i) (If no change,) how often?*
  - *(ii) (If yes,) in what way?*

HUSBAND: We never went anywhere. We took her to the drive-in movies a couple times. We'd ride around until she went to sleep. Early she wasn't too bad. As she got older we couldn't manage her in public at all.

WIFE: I used to go Wednesday nights to my club, and he'd go bowling one night a week, Thursday.

[The wife mentioned again the sister-in-law who helped. There were two daughters in this family.]

HUSBAND: Their ten- and twelve-year-old daughters had first suggested that they have Margaret for weekends so that we could get a rest. They would say, "Bring *this* dress when you bring her over and bring that one."

At first, it was kind of rough [at work].

WIFE: I guess he had it with him all the time. He used to call me up quite often.

HUSBAND: There's only the two of us working together; I had the kind of a job where I could leave the boiler house and go over and work on a machine. I was always wondering what was going on. Was my wife all right? It was mostly her I was concerned about. If I just had to stand tending the machine it would have driven me nuts.

We had both been going [to church] pretty regularly, and then with this trouble we stopped.

WIFE: Then my husband was working Sundays.

HUSBAND: That's a poor excuse. We should go more often.

Part II

Going Away to the Training School

1. How old was your child when you first considered Southbury Training School as a place for him?

(a) Had you considered any other solution earlier?
(b) How did you happen to hear about Southbury?
(c) What did you hear?

WIFE: Three and a half or four. We thought we would try to keep her home and train her.

2. Who suggested to you that you should send your child to Southbury Training School?

(a) Doctor?
(b) Schoolteacher?
(c) Social worker?
(d) Tester?
(e) Someone else?

WIFE: Dr. Samsel.

3. Who is the person who helped you most to make the decision to send your child to Southbury?

WIFE: When Dr. Samsel told us the second time and then walked away, there was a nice woman doctor who talked to us almost an hour about Southbury. She explained it, how much better she would be at Southbury. [They really worked it out themselves.]

4. What made you take the first step toward getting your child entered at Southbury Training School (putting his name on the list, that is)?

(a) Was there a crucial incident?
(b) How long did you think you could keep him home after you applied?

WIFE: I could not handle her any more.

HUSBAND: As she got older, my wife never got out with her. One morning I came out in the kitchen. There she was sitting on the shelf of the stove, teetering back and forth, letting her feet almost touch the hot stove top. She used to sit on that shelf. *(going over to the stove)* See how wobbly. That's something else I've got to fix around here. It's good to have the handle back on the refrigerator; we used to keep the handle up here, and the bolt that fastened it over in that drawer. Margaret would clean out the icebox. One time my wife caught her sitting on the ledge outside the window as though to wash the windows on the outside. Once in the summer when the oil wasn't on, she walked across the stove top and burned her foot on the gas burner.

WIFE: One time she had gone with her father in the car. He went into a store, thought he had left the car doors locked. She got out, ran across State Street in all the traffic. On the other side a woman caught her and held on to her tight so she couldn't get away. She said she realized something was wrong when Margaret didn't talk or answer her questions. Was my husband frantic!

HUSBAND: We were told it would take one or two years. I do not think my wife was really ready, even when we did put her on the list. Every day it seemed as though we couldn't hold out much longer.

WIFE: Six months after applying it got so bad I called Mrs. Simpson and asked her, "Oh, how much longer have we got to wait?"

HUSBAND: And then when we got the notice, we didn't know whether we wanted to admit her or not.

Do you remember the lights episode? One night my brother and his wife were here. Margaret brought a chair over in the middle of the kitchen floor and turned on the overhead light. Then we would turn it off. I don't know how many times she did it. We'd keep turning the light off and putting the chair back in the corner and she'd go back and get the chair, climb on it and turn the light back on. We were trying to tire her out so that she would sleep. She finally got so she staggered but she kept right on pushing the chair across the room and climbing up again to turn on the light.

5. Did some of your close relatives or friends oppose the decision to commit your child to the training school? Tell me about it.

HUSBAND: At the beginning they thought she would outgrow it. They'd say, "Don't worry about it. She will be all right." When they found out we were going to enter her in Southbury, they'd say, "It's the best thing."

6. After it was decided to have your child leave home, how did you manage while you were waiting?

(a) Was it physically or emotionally more difficult?

(b) Was it easier or harder after you had made the decision to commit him?

HUSBAND: The last six months were really hard.

WIFE: The last six months were much harder. Yes, it's a good thing that we put in the application. If we only knew what she wanted. [The husband also expressed his frustration at not being able to communicate with Margaret.]

7. While you were waiting, what was your greatest worry about your child's going to Southbury Training School?

(a) Did you have some fears concerning the type of people who might have charge of children in state institutions?

(b) Did you have some fears concerning the type of children your child would be put with?

(c) Did you feel that your child would get adequate care from the cottage workers?

HUSBAND: Sleeping mostly. We wondered what they would do with her nights.

WIFE: About her ever getting away!

HUSBAND: We can honestly say now that she's better off, but a week before she went away I wouldn't have said so.

WIFE: [Fears about personnel?] No, because we had made two visits, and I had met quite a few house girls and the house mothers. On a visit the house girls at 17 had taken Margaret into the building for a visit. Dr. Nubel took us up to 17, said, "It depends on her history but perhaps she will be there." No. 17 is a lovely cottage. Have you ever seen it? *(to interviewer)*

[Fears about other children?] No.

[Adequate care?] Yes.

8. After they told you there was a place ready for your child, did you postpone bringing him to Southbury? (If yes,) why?

HUSBAND: No.

WIFE: I wouldn't talk about it for a while after the notice came. Everyone asked if I had heard any bad news.

HUSBAND: We were hesitant but we didn't put it off.

9. When your child went to Southbury Training School, what did you hope that they would be able to do for him there? Did you expect that he might be able to return home to stay after training?

WIFE: Teach her to train herself and take care of herself.

HUSBAND: Quiet her down.

WIFE: It had taken us a good long time to realize that she couldn't be any more—that she couldn't be a normal child. Her eating habits aren't as good now.

HUSBAND: [Come home after training?] Yes, I think so. I thought eventually . . .

WIFE: I thought it would be a long time. I hoped—there's always hope.

10. Tell me about when you took him to Southbury for the first time.
(a) Who was with you? (your husband?)
(b) What did you do?
(c) Was there anything that happened that day that you especially remember?

WIFE: I wouldn't talk about it. Having a big family was hard. We said not to have anyone come before Margaret went to Southbury. But they all came anyway. And my mother was there all day. They were all saying good-bye to her.

HUSBAND: We sat here and looked at each other that day.

WIFE: Just we two went up. The doctor interviewed me at the hospital. My husband had Margaret for almost two hours in the car. The doctor asked me all those questions all over again. I didn't think it was necessary and told him so, for they had all the records from the New Haven Hospital. I could look out of the window and see them in the car, and knew that she was tearing the car apart.

HUSBAND: I didn't know how long she would be. If I had known, I could have taken Margaret for a ride. She was really upset that day. She was tearing everything apart.

WIFE: I was nervous as it was. The doctor told me to relax and I couldn't relax. If they had let us take her to the cottage and leave her and then come back for the interview to the hospital it wouldn't have been so bad.

11. How did you feel after you left your child there?
(a) How did your husband feel?
(b) Did you feel that you had "given your child up"?

HUSBAND: My wife cried all the way home.

WIFE: Coming home was worse. Coming in the house—it was so quiet. Nothing around. My little niece asked me when I got out of the car, "Where is Margaret?"

HUSBAND: (*to the interviewer*) At least we had this little guy to come home to. You didn't.

WIFE: I had to forget my troubles and think of him. That's the hardest part, to see her clothes around.

HUSBAND: My wife gave her dresses to her sister upstairs.

WIFE: That pretty gray dress! I've never seen that on her little girl. Maybe she feels it a little too.

[The husband seemed to be trying to cheer his wife up at these difficult questions by telling some anecdote of Margaret's mischief.] HUSBAND: The car keys! The set with all the keys to the plant! She was playing with them, then out the car window! I turned around and went back to look for them in the grass along the highway where I thought they went out. I looked and looked. Anyone coming along would have thought I was crazy. I never found them. Gee, I was mad.

[Given child up?] No, I don't think so. I knew I could go up and get her back again.

WIFE: No. Mrs. Johns told us that any time we felt like it, just climb in the car and come up. We're lucky; we're close to the school.

HUSBAND: (*to the interviewers*) Being parents yourselves makes it different. Anybody else coming in, it would be a cut-and-dried interview.

12. How long was it before you went up for your first visit? How did you pass the time?

WIFE: Only from Tuesday to Sunday. I knew I had to forget my troubles and think of Timmy at home.

13. How did you both feel after your first visit to your child in his cottage at Southbury?

(a) Did you feel encouraged or discouraged?
(b) (If encouraged,) what helped you to feel encouraged?
(c) (If discouraged,) what might have helped you to feel better?

HUSBAND: Very good.

WIFE: Encouraged.

HUSBAND: How clean!

WIFE: No, not just clean, but how happy she looked. She came walking down the corridor toward us smiling. She was all nicely dressed and smelled sweet.

Part III

Subsequent Experiences

1. How old is your child now?

WIFE: Six years old.

2. Do you go to visit him at Southbury?

WIFE: Yes.

3. Do you bring him home for visits?

WIFE: Yes.

4. How do you feel about Southbury as a training school?

HUSBAND: I do not see how it could be better. We only know about Cottage 17, but we have met personnel from all over the school, and we see how they keep the place.

WIFE: The best as far as we know. Of course we're speaking of Cottage 17.

5. What effect have the attractive buildings and grounds of Southbury Training School had on your feelings about your child's being there?

HUSBAND: The way they keep the place and things like that. It means a lot. That was one thing we often thought about—a four-story building with bars on the windows. That's how we pictured it.

WIFE: I had it pictured different. I thought it was beautiful.

6. How about the people at the cottage—what kind of people are they?
(a) Do you think they are warmly interested in the children?
(b) Did you feel any differently about them before? (If yes,) what has happened to make you feel differently?

WIFE: Yes.

HUSBAND: Yes, if I bring her back late, they still have something for her before she goes to bed, milk and cookies. A popcorn party they had one night. They wouldn't do things like that unless they liked the kids.

7. Have you had any talks about your child with the staff or the people in the office at Southbury since his admission?

(a) How did you find them—what kind of people are they?

(b) Did you feel differently about them before? (If yes,) what has happened to make you feel differently?

[No contacts]

HUSBAND: I'd like to know her improvement, and what to do on that. I'd like to know what they have found from testing her.

WIFE: I always ask at the cottage as to how she's doing. I still want to know her progress too.

8. Do you feel that Southbury Training School actually carries out the belief that every child has a right to receive training, if only to help him take care of himself?
(Do not ask parents of infirm children.) If a child cannot be taught a trade, do you think it right to have him mopping up, picking up papers, or washing dishes?

HUSBAND: That we do not know. I think they are trying to.

WIFE: They are trying. They say they could do better with a few more personnel. I think it makes a difference with the child.

HUSBAND: What she needs mostly is attention. They tell us not to rush it.

9. What do you think would have happened if your child had not gone to Southbury Training School:

(a) To your family at home?

(b) To your child?

WIFE: [Happen to family?] I think my husband and I . . .

HUSBAND: (*laughing bitterly*) Turn on the gas jets.

WIFE: I don't think I could have stood it.

HUSBAND: It was either my wife or her.

BROTHER-IN-LAW: Their nerves would have cracked.

HUSBAND: I was getting so at times I was afraid to go to work and leave my wife alone.

WIFE: That was the farthest from my thoughts. I would have been afraid.

HUSBAND: [Happen to child?] She'd still be playing that Perry Como record.

WIFE: I do not know. I have often wondered. She has quieted down. They say there is an uncanny bond between those children, but that if you put them with normal children they do not do so well. I think that she's happier at school. They're not after her as much as we were. There wouldn't be any curtains to pull down!

10. Are you glad you sent your child to Southbury, or are you sorry you sent him? Why?

WIFE: Glad.

11. Do you wish your child had been admitted later or earlier than he was? Why might that have been better?

WIFE: Earlier. I think so. I wish we had put her name in earlier. She couldn't have been admitted any earlier.

HUSBAND: We were lucky. If she had been home another year it wouldn't have mattered; we were at the point where it wouldn't have mattered to us.

WIFE: But it wouldn't have been fair to the baby.

12. I asked you a while ago, "What did you hope they would be able to do for your child at Southbury?"
(a) What do you now think they have done for him?
(b) What do you hope that he will be able to do?

HUSBAND: They have quieted her down. She's more able to run in and out. She has more freedom than she was able to have at home. There hasn't been enough time to tell yet. She has been up there just a year.

BROTHER-IN-LAW: You can know that they have helped Margaret because she is glad when she goes back after a visit.

HUSBAND: Yes, she knows she's back; she goes back eagerly. At home she wouldn't come into the house from the car.

[Hope she will do?] Dr. Samsel told us, "You're not going to teach her too much, even toilet training. She's six years old now, and not even a year mentally."

13. Do you think Southbury Training School could do more for your child than it is now doing?

HUSBAND: No, not in her particular case. Dr. Samsel told us, "Take care of her, see that she doesn't get hurt. Train her? No, you're just going to train yourself."

14. Do you visit with the people in the cottage and talk over your child's progress and problems with them?

HUSBAND: Yes, frequently. We ask them every visiting time. They're very sociable, every one of them. One of the nurses said to us, "She's quite active, isn't she?"

WIFE: Now she has the run of the place. But at first they had a girl assigned to her all the time.

15. Do you feel the training school accepts your child as an individual person?

HUSBAND: It's more like a family. It is more than just personal or individual. They all call Mrs. Johns "Mother."

16. Do you think your child does have a real feeling of belonging at the training school—is attached to it as to a home (away from home)?

[The mother is bothered by this question. But she is reassured when we stress the difference between a second home and a second family.]

HUSBAND: Yes, as far as she is able to. I know she likes it. She is more at home there than she is here.

WIFE: She has more freedom. She's content.

17. Do you think the training school actually tries to help children keep close family ties with the parents?
(a) (If yes,) how?
(b) (If no,) how do they fail in this?

HUSBAND: Oh, definitely. Because when she first went up there we got a letter the very next day after she went to the hospital with a little temperature. They told us to feel free to come when we wanted. They do help us to feel good when we are there. The fifth Sunday we have gone up and they treat us royally. [The first and third Sundays of the month are visiting days.]

WIFE: We have never brought anyone up but that they have shown them around and made them welcome.

HUSBAND: And the social worker came down and talked to my wife and explained their routine. We were surprised when she came down.

18. Do you now feel that "you have given your child up"?

HUSBAND: No, definitely not.

WIFE: Never.

19. Do you think Southbury Training School is helping your child enough so that he may be able to:
(a) Come home to stay?
(b) Come home for long visits?

HUSBAND: No, we thought earlier if she got to the point where she understood, and we could handle her, she could come home. We know it's impossible now. We tried it. A lot of times when we started to think maybe we could have kept her home, we have her home for a day and can see soon enough that it would not work.

20. A while back, I asked if you went to visit your child at Southbury. You said no. *Have you found out this works better? Why?*

OR

21. A while back, I asked you if you went to visit your child at Southbury. You said yes. *About how often does someone go up to visit?*

WIFE: Every Visiting Sunday plus sometimes a fifth Sunday.

22. Who usually goes to see your child?
(a) Do you take your other children to visit? Do they want to go?
(b) Do you take anyone else, such as relatives, friends, neighbors?

[Both parents and Timmy go. Timmy looks forward to it. He gets excited. They usually take someone else, someone from the family.]

WIFE: We have a list, and check their names off as we take them up there.

23. What do you usually do on visits to your child at the training school?

HUSBAND: We take her for a ride off the grounds. [He had said earlier that he had never thought he would get to know one part of the state so well.] We went camping at Lake Waramaug State Park and had her up for the day a couple of times. Not on weekends—it's too crowded then.

[In bad weather they stay in the cottage. They tried a picnic with a lot of relatives, but it wasn't successful because Margaret got "nervous."]

HUSBAND: Timmy said to her when she was just grunting: "What's the matter, Margaret? Did we get you up?" And he will say, "Daddy is going to get you ice cream," and "Hey, Margaret, shake hands."

24. Do you:
(a) Usually visit in the cottage?
(b) Usually bring him outside the cottage?
(c) Ever have a picnic for him on the school grounds?
(d) Ever take him to the Gate House for ice cream?
(e) Do other things on the school grounds?
(f) Take him for a ride just by yourselves?
(g) Take him to picnic places or playgrounds?

(h) Take him to friends' homes?
(i) Take him to stores and restaurants?
(j) Take him to other places off the grounds?

[They checked (a), (b), (d), and (f). Margaret won't stay in a restaurant. They find it better not to take too many people.]

HUSBAND: The less company the better time she has. She sometimes falls asleep when we are alone in the car, and if she falls asleep, that's fine; that's like a normal family on a Sunday ride with the kids. Everybody picks her up; they grab her; there are too many people in the car when we take the relatives. We have to keep feeding her cookies and potato chips to quiet her down when there are too many visiting her.

25. Why do you go to visit your child?

HUSBAND: (*simply*) She's our child. Why do you go to visit yours?

WIFE: (*disturbed*) *Why* do I go! [Interviewer, placatingly: "Because you love her!"] She is my daughter, that's all; and I still say two weeks is not often enough to see her.

They say, "You are lucky that your daughter doesn't cry when you leave her." I must say I'd like her to cry just once to see that emotion, and that she knows I am her mother.

26. A while back, you folks said that you didn't bring your child home for visits. Have you found out that it's better not to?

OR

27. (If home visits) when was the last time your child was home on a visit?
(a) How often does he come?
(b) About how long does he stay?

HUSBAND: The day before Christmas. There was too much going on Christmas Day.

WIFE: [She visits four or five times a year.]

HUSBAND: Just for the day. Mrs. Johns has said it is too much and might risk her routine to have her home longer.

28. What things do you do when your child is home on a visit?

HUSBAND: We took her home once and did not tell anyone in the family. My brother-in-law gave her a haircut. We had a quiet time at home, and then took her back. That was a good visit.

Another time, on my wife's birthday, I told her I had to work; and I went up and got Margaret at Southbury and brought her home nice and early. My wife was still in bed. You should have seen her head pop up out of that bed when she saw Margaret.

WIFE: The less company we have the better fun she will have at home. It is easier taking her to friends' and relatives' homes; we can pop in and out. Our families have ten kids and seven kids, a lot of relatives. We bring her home for a haircut. One time she got one by mistake up there and Mrs. Johns came to the door and said, "Oh, Mrs. Fall, I've got bad news for you; they went and cut her hair."

29. When your child is home on a visit, do you:
(a) Have people in to see him?
(b) Try to find playmates for him?
(c) Take him calling on friends?
(d) Take him shopping?
(e) Take him to neighborhood social doings such as a child's birthday party?
(f) Take him to public functions such as church entertainments?
(g) Do other things?

[They checked a and c on the list.]

30. Do you find yourself comfortable now talking with folks outside the family about your child and the training school?
(a) Whom do you talk with?
(i) Good friends?
(ii) Neighbors?
(iii) Other parents of retarded children?
(iv) Casual acquaintances?
(v) Other people?
(b) What do you tell them?

[Before question 30 was asked, the wife volunteered the following to the interviewers:]

WIFE: To us these questions are just the kind of questions you want to answer.

HUSBAND: You put them in a way that we do not mind answering.

WIFE: Yes.

HUSBAND: It's okay now. Everyone you speak to knows something about Southbury; someone in the family or a friend's up there. [They checked all the list of people.]

WIFE: I tell them it is the best place for her; and I am glad they have a place for children like that, and that they take wonderful care of her.

31. As a family, would you say that you are more happy, or less happy than you were before your child went to Southbury? Why?

HUSBAND: Happy for her sake. We couldn't have her home the way she was.

WIFE: (*hesitates*) We are settled down. We're having a home life we never had before. I'd still like to see her running around though.

HUSBAND: When we do have her home though, we wonder how we ever did it.

32. (Ask only of young families.) How do you feel now about having more children?

(a) (Ask of small families) Have you thought of adopting a child?

(b) Have you taken any steps toward an adoption?

HUSBAND: Shh!!

WIFE: (*very firm*) I'd like to have more.

HUSBAND: I'd like her to have more.

WIFE: I *have* to have another one.

33. What's been the effect of your child's trouble on the way you've gotten along with your relatives over this period of time?

(a) How do you feel toward them now?

(b) Has their attitude toward your child changed?

(c) How do they feel now about your child's being at the training school?

[Other relatives in the room during this question may have restrained answering.]

HUSBAND: All I can say we can make our visits more often. We never got out at all. We never went visiting.

BROTHER-IN-LAW: You taught us that those kids up there need help.

HUSBAND: They [relatives] are all quite approving except my grandmother. Everybody else feels all right about it.

WIFE: Last summer they had Margaret out in the sun a lot up there. She got a wonderful tan. His grandmother thought that was terrible.

34. Just what effect has this trouble had on your family finances?

(a) Did you have a great deal of expense?

(b) Did it change what you spent your money for?

(c) Have you or the other children had to do without because of the retarded child?

(d) Has it affected their chances for an education?

(e) Has there been a change in jobs?

(f) Is the husband more satisfied in his work now since admission?

[Not a great deal of effect on family finances.
No heavy medical expenses.
Gasoline for the long evening rides.
No more expenses for Margaret than it would have been for a normal child.]

WIFE: She had dungarees and a polo shirt instead of dresses and movies.

HUSBAND: I bought a better car so as to get to Southbury.

[They did not feel they had had to do without, finance-wise. No change in jobs, regular raises.]

HUSBAND: [Satisfied in work?] Oh, yes, sure.

WIFE: He doesn't call me up any more.

HUSBAND: I called you up yesterday to see what we had for supper!

35. Now that your child is settled at Southbury:

(a) How active have you become in club doings and neighborhood affairs?

(b) What else do you do for recreation now?

(c) How about your church attendance?

WIFE: We do not go out much even now.

HUSBAND: We feel free to, whether we do or not.

WIFE: Yes.

HUSBAND: Just climb in the car and go visit someone—that is new to us.

WIFE: We get a baby sitter easier.

HUSBAND: Just to be able to read the paper through or watch a television program all the way through, or to have a meal in peace.

Not back to it [church] yet. [We should, said the husband earlier.]

36. What are your hopes and plans for yourselves and the children at home?

WIFE: We have ideas about a house.

HUSBAND: We look forward to vacations more now. My wife wants to go to Canada.

WIFE: Oh, I'd love a house.

37. Have you been to parents' meetings at Southbury—the Home and School Association?

(a) Are you interested in the Association now?

(b) Do you think it helps some?

[Not yet to meeting. They have been to the Open House at the school.]

38. How about the ARC group near you—have you been to the meetings there? Do you belong?

[They have been to meetings. They do not belong.]
[The husband came back at the end to the statement he had made earlier.] There was more in that association for local—for kids that can go to school, for trainable mongoloids in the city.

39. In what ways do you think parents' groups could be of most help to you as parents?

HUSBAND: Oh, gee, I do not know. To help each other, in a case where some parents do not have automobiles.
WIFE: For things they need at the school. Help each other out.

40. What would you think of the idea of getting together occasionally with a few other parents and a professional person and just talking over your mutual problems?

HUSBAND: I could see it—something like that. More with a doctor. Someone familiar with Southbury especially.

Section I

Chapter 1

The Impact of Discovery

Discovery of retardation had been immediate in at least one case. The husband had been apprised of the child's condition and the prognosis the day he was born. With the wife's parents he had been planning the placement of the child in a private hospital. They did not risk telling the wife, who after a very difficult delivery had been too ill to care for the infant for three weeks.

Then the wife, all eager to go down to the hospital and get her baby, was detoured to her parents' home, where her mother broke the news to her while her husband and her father went out into the yard. The wife remembered:

> She said evasively, "He is not a well child." Why I said it I do not know—I guess I had a sixth sense, and I said, "Not a mongolian idiot!" She said, "Yes." I went into hysterics, and I couldn't wait to get to the hospital. I couldn't wait! They didn't want me to go, and they tried to stop me, but I had to find out for myself. The minute I saw him—he was scrawny and looked so hopelessly pathetic, not like the same baby I delivered. When he was born, I had said to the nurse, "Aren't I wonderful?" I thought he was a beautiful baby when he was born. I wondered why my husband didn't get too enthusiastic about all my plans and hopes for the baby those three weeks. I couldn't understand his reaction. . . .
>
> I was hysterical when I first heard about it from my mother. My mother never picked him up from the day he was born. I kept saying I was going to keep him home as long as I could do him any good. It was against the advice of many friends. At first I really didn't know what I was up against. My mother never understood it either. She told somebody that he was going to be deaf, dumb, and blind. . . .
>
> I was in bed three days more after that. I felt so badly for him; I lay there in bed at home and resented the children laughing or crying outside: "Why had God deserted me? Why am I being punished? Why does He punish this innocent? It shouldn't be inflicted on an innocent child." I was so set for him; I was so anxious for him! You have an immediate protective instinct when your child is born. . . . A friend of mine had a kid born the same day as he;

and when I see someone who is eight years old, and when the kids here his age first go to school—those things hurt. I enjoyed him very much; it was no effort to love him. He was very sweet, and he needed help so much I hated to leave him up there.

For the bewildered family who experienced early discovery, immediate placement in a private nursery or "children's hospital" was the customary recommendation by the attending pediatrician or the doctors at the hospital. Along with the bleak prognosis came the strong suggestion that it would be better not to bring this child into the home. This advice was not meant unkindly; it was doubtless predicated on the expectancy of a very brief lifetime. (But through modern medicine more and more such children are surviving each year.)

There was some variation in how other families found out and who first told them about their child's retardation. In several instances quite clear as to clinical implications, parents brought a child home from the hospital all unknowing. The doctors just hadn't told them. They got their first knowledge months later, unexpected and with harsh abruptness.

One wife described finding out about her mongoloid child:

At one year, not until the first two teeth came in. These teeth came in in a point and ulcerated so I took her to the baby clinic at New Haven Hospital. I had had her to a doctor that whole year, Dr. DeLeito the pediatrician; but he didn't tell me. At the New Haven Hospital clinic I thought they would look in her mouth at her teeth. They looked not at her mouth, but at her fingers, different parts of her body. Then finally one doctor took me into this little room and told me what kind of a child Carlotta was, and how she would never walk or talk and always have the mind of a six-year-old child. I just couldn't believe it when they told me; I just couldn't believe it.

There had been some warning early:

The first thing, she did not have any instinct on sucking. She was born 9 pounds, went down to 6 pounds in a few weeks. Then we tried the bottle. Dr. O'Connell gave her a bottle with a pump on it; then she started to pick up very fast.

For a majority of these families the discovery was a longer process. It spanned many months from the moment of first suspicion through to the realization of the fact of retardation. One family experienced discovery at "about two years old":

[*Husband*] We talked a great deal with Dr. Robinson, the pediatrician. He has said to us since that it has been a matter of chagrin that he did not discover it earlier. Arthur was not walking or talking. [*Wife*] He was so normal otherwise and healthy. From his physical appearance there was no clue.

Although they suspected that all was not right with their young child by his first birthday, most parents did not learn of the retardation until about age two. Then another year, even two, might pass before the full implication of his severe retardation was brought home to them.

There were children who had had some clinical history at birth, but no suggestion then of mental impairment. Thereafter, their parents were preoccupied with illnesses in infancy or some physical disability which obscured from them the mental deficiency. These parents who had been struggling, with some success they felt, to remedy a physical weakness or handicap bore very ill the suggestion that this cherished child should be sent away, that he was too defective to care for at home.

There were cases, too, where *nothing* had happened at birth or in early infancy to give them or their doctor any premonition that their child was to be so sadly different. Only in retrospect could these families recall any items of behavior during infancy that had seemed at all strange. These particular children were usually healthy, active, big. They responded to affection and attention. They laughed, were high-spirited, and even their exuberance was more a cause of pride and amusement than misgiving. Some proximate explanation could always be found for their occasional storminess. They ate with gusto (but were a little finicky about food). They started walking on time; they had excellent large-motor coordination. They *were* slow in talking; but they loved to be read to, to listen to music; and some showed signs of a prodigious memory. It was indeed a very gradual thing for the parents to come to realize the significance of differences in behavior between their child and other children of the same age. Particularly was this so if this was a first child and there was not close contact with other young children. Only as they compared him with his normal age-mates did they realize how far he was lagging behind—in speech, habit-training, emotional and perhaps also now even physical development.

Parents acquired an uneasy awareness that their child could not solve problems, could not figure things out like the others, that he was hard to teach, "but what he learned he would do no other." They were sure now that he was a little slow, but there was still no conception that he would be *ever* slower than the other children. They were preoccupied with little specific worries, such as "how could he be trained to walk safely along the road to school when it came time for him to start kindergarten next fall?" They might well be the last ones to realize the gravity of their child's defect; and he might approach school age before their discovery was complete. Then a kindergarten or nursery school teacher rather than the doctor might be the first professional to tell them. If their relatives or close friends had an earlier knowledge, usually they waited for the parents to realize it.

There was a common quality, however, in how the parents felt when they were told that their child was severely retarded. Almost always their first response was shocked disbelief. Even if they had come to the clinic with strong premonitions, they could scarcely accept the doctors' authoritative prognosis. A late discovery might be especially painful for the parents:

> He was three or three and a half. We took him because we thought he was deaf, but all we got was a letdown! We had a pediatrician, but he didn't tell us until we pushed it, then he sent us to the hospital clinic. . . . I asked, "How is he going to sit for them to teach him in school?" They said, "He is never going to school." . . . I felt so much alone. . . . This has been an awful issue! I never had such an issue in my life. I went up to New Haven Hospital with him and paid my money, and there were students all around, and they tried to get me to talk. I paid a lot to go to doctors. I didn't think I was a guinea pig. I do not think I was treated right.

Parents vividly recalled their feelings on this dark day, their actions and thoughts after the doctor told them. One mother walked and carried her toddler five miles home from the city "so as not to see people on the bus," or perhaps to postpone reality—it would not be true until she had gotten home with the child. Another drove slowly over the highway to her home in a neighboring city, photographing in her mind's eye every prosaic detail along the route. Ten years later she still relived this journey.

Often feelings were expressed through a sharp recollection of their thoughts on that stark occasion. Years had passed for each of these families, yet they still remembered. Said a husband:

> My wife and her mother came back from the Child Development Clinic. We sat here; and her mother talked to me—but it couldn't happen! I just thought about that trip back to town the night he was born, and how I would play ball with him, and go hunting like my dad and I. Just the week before, somebody wanted to give me a Shetland pony for Charles; but we only had an apartment on Grand Avenue. I lost half of myself.

A wife remembered:

> We came home and sat down, and we both cried. It was just a complete shock, just the end of the world! The addition was going up in back, and we had some new chairs for the living room. We said, "Isn't it too bad we started all those things because this is the end; life is never going to be the same anymore—what is the sense?"

This sort of feeling may have been quite common. What grieved them most were the goals foregone, the hopes never to be realized for the child. It was the thought (several fathers expressed it) that "she could never grow up to lead a normal life." They did not recall worrying then over how they could manage to care for the child at home in the near future. The prospect of the need later on to separate the child from the family scarcely entered their consciousness. They might have heard the words, "Care for her now. Send her to Southbury when she is six," but they could not listen then; they would not comprehend. It was as if they hoped to soften the despair of what they felt by reserving for yet a while longer any acceptance of the facts and the steps they would have to take.

Parents were not comfortable at discovery time talking about the problem of their retarded child, especially if his physical condition was deteriorating or his behavior had become erratic. They felt that the parents of normal children just couldn't ever understand. Sometimes when they did make an effort to talk about it, friends and relatives would respond by minimizing the trouble, perhaps at the very time when the parents were trying to accept the harsh prognosis. Asked if she felt comfortable talking about her daughter's problem, one wife said:

> No, I did not! I tried to tell people about it. They all tried to be encouraging and that hurt; so I quit it. Once in a while they said, "Oh, I'm sorry," which was better; a little sympathy, that would help. But the others—I could no longer bear it, so I quit trying to talk. My husband's mother would not believe anything that was unfortunate; it just couldn't be, she thought.

At discovery desolate parents had to ask the questions: "Why did this ever happen? Why did it happen to us?" Even parents with a deep religious faith were perplexed and a little rebellious:

> We felt very bad about it, as any other parent would. We couldn't understand why it happened to a child in a family where they would have the right care and to the mother and father who wanted him. Beautiful healthy children are left to run barefooted on the streets. . . . This was a son which my husband and I wanted so badly. As good as girls are, they are always for the mother. We felt bad, our only son, that it should happen to a son which he had wanted so badly as a companion for years to come.

At discovery most parents were deeply concerned about possible causes of mental defect in their child. About half of the families tended to put the blame on something specific, a definite illness in pregnancy, birth trauma, or postnatal accident. This seemed reasonable enough. German measles or other acute illness in early pregnancy might well have been the cause of developmental anomalies in a child who at birth appeared normal. Convulsive disorders and some forms of cerebral palsy might reasonably be attributed to a traumatic birth experience. Hospitals were grossly understaffed, doctors and nurses badly overworked in the years when most of these children were born. There were two cases where the retardation seemed definitely the result of illness in late infancy.

The other half of the sample parents had nothing so specific to go on. Some of these readily accepted the explanation that "something went wrong in the making." Some fixed on a minor accident or vague illness during pregnancy and were halfway convinced that this was the cause: "I had to know the cause even if that was not it!"

Usually, parents somehow grew sadly accustomed to their child's being retarded; speculation about causes seldom occupied them. Perhaps they took cold comfort in the thought: "There are more than 70 known causes of mental retardation; what is the use of wondering about it?"

There were good reasons, however, for some of these parents to continue to seek out a cause. Young families, especially if other pregnancies were unsuccessful, wanted to be reassured that these were all accidents, that it was not a matter of heredity or reproductive defect. Older families with teenage children were concerned about their future. If only it could be established through medical evidence, hospital records, that the retarded child's brain damage was probably caused by birth trauma or other accident, then they could effectively deny any imputation that their family stock was somehow tainted.

The pediatrician or child psychologist could be of great help at discovery time, leading sensitive parents to put the matter of causation in proper perspective. It did seem that parents could more constructively and more effectively plan care for their retarded child and their other children too when they had succeeded in satisfactorily settling this matter of causation.

Few parents in the study group had acquired any valid knowledge of retardation before it happened to them. (Indeed, some foreign-born parents denied that mental retardation ever occurred among the people of their native land.) They had all grown up in the hush-hush days and had only casual peripheral contacts with families where this problem had existed.

There were a few individual parents who had experienced a closer connection with this problem, but they did not have useful knowledge, just unhappy memories of the social hardships for the families involved.

One mother, a college graduate and former social worker, had sufficient background to help her own difficult planning. She wrote letters to the proper agencies; she knew the resources available in the community; she got the cooperation of the VNA (Visiting Nurses Association) and the town. Another mother, interested in the problem through psychology courses in college, had visited Vineland and Letchworth Village as a student. But she said:

> There was only one instance that I knew of personally. . . . It's quite a different matter when it's somebody you know. I had a friend who had such a child. This is quite different from visiting a school.

This mother actually anticipated the doctor's first suggestion of placement:

> Actually we saw it ourselves; nobody shocked us. We still kept hoping that something would happen until she was past two, but we knew it wouldn't. I was the one who recognized that she would need Southbury. I said one time to Dr. Robinson, "Hadn't we better just apply for Southbury?" It was getting to be so hard on the rest of us. We had the other baby.

A few parents did follow professional advice as promptly as they could. One mother sought corroboration from other doctors and then applied quickly for Southbury:

> I wanted to give the child a fair chance, so even if it did cost us a few dollars it was worth seeing other doctors, but then they all pointed to the same answer. I went to the three best doctors I could get, plus my own doctor, and then to the big man again. I knew he wasn't normal.

Another family deliberated over the doctor's prognosis and advice and tried to work the problem out:

> We discussed then whether it was best to try to deal with it at home or whether a school was the answer—and if it was a school, then what school? . . . It took us a little time to wonder and weigh it in our own minds, though.

Those few families who did apply promptly after thinking the matter through together benefited from this early application. But this occurred only when the professional recommendation was unequivocal, their confidence in the doctors complete, and when the parents themselves had moved toward the same conclusion.

However, most families at discovery fully intended to keep their handicapped child at home into the indefinite future; this was what most parents thought should be done. Some felt it was a moral duty: "You're the mother and I'm the father and we've got to suffer. My kid isn't going anywhere." Or "It was our problem and we were going to take care of her."

Parents rarely qualified this intention to make a place for a defective child in an otherwise normal family setting. In the early years some of these children required no more care than a normal baby:

Up until that time [age two and a half] she was just a loving baby; she didn't get into anything. She didn't walk until 22 months. She just crawled around and played. She acted like a younger child. Where I placed her, that's where I found her. Really the trouble didn't start until the second child came.

They buoyed up their hopes. Possibly the doctor had somehow erred: "I didn't think she could be that bad." Or "I didn't believe him. I thought he was wrong; he could have made a mistake, too." They thought that "when she was fifteen she might be ten mentally," not that "she would get to five [or two] and stay there."

Some parents because of their own feelings could not avail themselves of professional help at discovery. A mother recalled an early visit to the doctor who later was able to help her through commitment:

I had gone to him myself when Wesley was a baby, and he had said, "You're too nervous to nurse a baby." That was at three months, but I didn't tell him what was wrong at that early time. I just couldn't. I wasn't ready. I started to; I wanted to; but I just couldn't bring myself to.

There was one family whose little girl proved to have cerebral palsy. Because she was such an attractive infant, interested in her environment, the parents for a while discounted their suspicions. But at a year the child had not yet sat up, so guided by their family physician, they sought out a specialist, "a pediatrician who had a great deal of experience in this line." The couple recalled this consultation:

[*Wife*] He said she was severely retarded; he estimated four months mental age. He said, "Prepare yourselves for the fact that she will not get through life independently, that she will have to have institutional care." [*Husband*] This doctor had laid it on the line for Roosevelt's secretary's kid. He was in the Blue Book. He diagnosed Martha's case while we were sitting there in the office waiting. He was sharp but honest. [*Wife*] He probably showed us more attention than he would have with someone else. He went out of his way to explain it to us. We were just 24 years old with our first baby.

[*Husband*] I didn't believe it; I went on for five years not really believing it. . . . My wife ran down the stairs crying with the baby. I paid the doctor. [*Wife*] A girl friend and her husband had driven us down to the doctor's. I was crying so hard I couldn't tell them what was the matter. [*Husband*] I remember it very distinctly. It was something we both suspected and here was a fellow who told us the truth. I think we believed it, but what could you do? Before Martha was born, we had great plans for our first child. That day we thought about some of the things we had planned for her. . . .

[*Wife*] When we went back to our family physician he tried to explain to us how she probably would be in the future; he de-

> scribed a spastic [cerebral palsy]. [*Husband*] Actually at the time she didn't do anything that bothered me. Later she had these convulsions that were terrific. [*Wife*] One reason I found it so hard to accept was that she did not have any of the appearance of a retarded child. [*Husband*] In repose she was normal-looking.
>
> [*Wife*] We used to stand her down on her feet—with her braces on. We would stand back of her and kick first one foot and then the other. One night she took one step. [*Husband*] That was the biggest thing in my life, that night. [*Wife*] It got so she could keep it up longer than we; she would go on a tour all over the room; we'd pause at the desk and she would look into the wastebasket. I don't know about my husband, but I was fooling myself back then. [*Husband*] I think we all were. I don't think my father would ever admit she was retarded. She seemed to be making real progress until about a year later when the convulsion equivalents struck again. . . . [*Wife*] When my husband and I had talked it over and accepted it a little bit, we said, "Maybe someday an institution for her," but then we both put institution out of our minds.

The typical set of parents in the study realized that their child was "different" before one year. They learned of his retardation sometime when he was two. Sensibly, they had confidence in the doctors, and to a point they accepted the prognosis. But they were going to keep *their* retarded child at home. They were going to set up the home so that they could take care of him. They didn't realize how wide would become the gap between their child's behavior and that of his age-mates who were normal.

Chapter 2

The Severely Retarded Child

The severely retarded child functions at a minimal level, below that required of a full participating member of society. Problem-solving and abstract learning are beyond him. He might learn to dress himself except for tying his shoes. He might count to six and sing a little song through memory and repetition; but he cannot master the simplest arithmetic concepts, nor can he handle the symbols for reading a primer. He cannot organize his experiences. His ability to communicate what he does know is limited, so his social interaction with other people in his environment is circumscribed.

If he is below the range of *trainable,* profoundly retarded, requiring complete custody and imprisoned by his infirmity, then his relation to his world is limited to pain-or-pleasure responses. If he survives he grows, getting heavier and perhaps stronger, experiencing an irregular maturation. The gap between such a child and his normal age-mates widens each year:

> Benjy at five years was still a baby of six months. When I'd finally get the baby to sleep, Benjy would wake. We had to lie down on the bed with him until he would sleep because of his bouncing. No crib would hold him. . . . (We were only away from him two times in five years. You *have* to get away sometimes.) Benjy was wearing a size 14 when he went up there, still does. He was so strong, but he couldn't help you to carry him. He wouldn't hold on, but would flip himself back when you lifted.

The thirty children in this study group comprised a variety of clinical types and classifications. Three frequent categories were mongolism, cerebral palsy, and brain damage, the last a popular term roughly equivalent to the clinician's "undifferentiated cranial anomalies." Along with mongolism there was apt to be found congenital heart disorder or respiratory weakness. Associated with the cerebral palsy were seizures of varying severity, digestive troubles, and sometimes paralysis. With the brain-damaged or undifferentiated there was a wide range of impairment from a diffuse cerebral damage, accompanied by normal appearance and health but erratic behavior, to a severe complex of convulsive disorders or degenerative central nervous system disease.

The severely retarded child may be described also in terms of the behavior and care problems he presents. At least three variables are involved: (1) the relative deficiency in intelligence, (2) the degree of physical impairment or lack of function, and (3) the general long-term medical outlook for him. Parents in their descriptions laid equal stress on their retarded child's behavior and his condition. Both of these adversely affected the operation of the home and the functioning of the family, sometimes altering its very structure.

A placid infirm child who could be kept comfortable with routine bedside care would still occupy an inordinate share of a mother's time and attention, confining her to the home unless there were older children or a close relative to provide regular relief. An older infirm child who had to be lifted and carried was quite difficult to care for. So also was the palsied one whose limbs flailed uncontrollably as his mother tried to feed him, or the child whose retardation was complicated by severe seizures or susceptibility to infection. And the burden of the care was always heavier if the child was stigmatized.

A very ill and suffering infirm child would be the complete focus of attention of all the adults in the family:

> [*Mother*] I do not know how the poor little thing has a brain after all those seizures. They were murderous. To think there were four big people and we couldn't do a thing to help her. She would be asleep and would have a seizure in her legs; it would wake her up and she would cry pitifully. All the family would be up and walk the floor all night with her. Only at night she would get her seizures. [*Grandmother*] I'd hear them up about 2:30 in the morning. I'd come up and my husband soon behind me. We took turns holding her. [*Mother*] Phil [the younger brother] never heard her, and he slept in the same room with her. Timothy [the older brother] would hear her and come down. . . . My husband would try very hard to get me to stay in bed; but I wanted him to rest because he had to work all day. My husband used to be punchy from lack of sleep. [*Grandmother*] Both of them were trying to spare the other. . . . I often wondered how I survived lifting and holding that baby so much. I *willed* to live to help her a little bit. After Naomi went to Southbury, it didn't matter. . . . That one child would have ruined everyone else's life around here . . . those two young boys!

Ambulatory children of a higher mental level and some social competence, whom their families could enjoy, might be highly susceptible to illness. Customary childhood diseases were never mild cases for them. This meant that at frequent intervals the entire family would have to adapt to illness of crisis proportions. A couple recalled:

[*Wife*] Anthony weighed 9 pounds at birth, and only 14 at a year. We nearly lost him at eight months with strep throat. [*Husband*] He had a nice speaking voice until age four, when he had the croup severely. He was on the danger list for seven days at the hospital then. [*Wife*] We were always so worried with his heart. The tonsil operation at five was a fifty-fifty chance; but they said that if he did not have them out he would not live anyway. [*Husband*] They had every nun in St. Raphael's Hospital down at the operating room saying the Rosary and praying; and Dr. Murphy was saying, "I don't think this boy is going to live. Where is the father? Where is the mother?" That was when I walked into the hospital!

A strong healthy child below mid-range of the trainable might, through erratic and hyperactive behavior, constitute an arduous problem of care and protection:

He was always on top of you! He would flush the toilet, open the gas jets, "make" the coffee. How many boxes of soap chips he would throw down the drain "washing the dishes." I could not go to the toilet—he would run out!

Another mother recalled:

You couldn't keep anything nice around the house. She would pull everything out of the refrigerator before we'd get up. . . . You'd need a truck to move the wreckage out. . . . She would stay up until one or two o'clock, and then she would be up again by three or four o'clock in the morning.

The father added:

She didn't require much rest for the amount of energy she used. She would listen to the music all night; sit on the sofa and bang her head on the back of the wall, keeping time almost to the music. If you held her on your lap, she wouldn't stay still. . . . She seemed to get as strong as a bull overnight. I always thought myself pretty strong, but there were nights I could scarcely hold her.

There was yet another instance:

He was too active; he was hard to handle, to care for. You couldn't let him out of your sight; you couldn't trust him to do anything; he might get hurt. You had to be too careful! You must watch him at all times. He would break dishes, cut himself. He would climb trees, but wouldn't know enough to hold on; he would fall. . . . I'd be awfully nervous. He'd get me down, because I was the only one who could take care of him. I got so I wouldn't dare go out with him, or leave him at home [alone] either.

Evidently, it was more than a matter of the retarded child's requiring so large a share of his parents' time and effort. There was also the strain because of the perpetual uncertainty. The retarded child's behavior just couldn't be predicted. Sometimes a child might show a near-normal response to the outside environment; and sometimes there might be a tantrum over some happening they couldn't anticipate. At any time, the child's seizures and illnesses would upset a precarious balance.

Besides the uncertainty, there was the fact of stigma as a source of strain. This would keep to a minimum interaction between the retarded child and any beyond the immediate family. It might put the home in isolation; certainly it would isolate the mother. A retarded child might be severely stigmatized in physical appearance "so that it would hurt people to look at him." The flailing of limbs, the uncontrollable physical activity of the cerebral palsied child, could be a disturbing sight. Sometimes a healthy, physically capable child of normal appearance would become excited and hyperactive when unable to handle the stimuli in an unaccustomed situation. Such a child's tantrums at age three would excite sympathy from outsiders and efforts to understand him. But tantrums and irrational behavior in a nine-year-old are a distressful mark upon the child—and a mark that sets apart his family as different.

The severely retarded child strongly influenced the functioning of the family while he remained at home. Both his medical condition and his actions forced family members to modify their roles and adapt to him. Many of these retarded children became the central focus of family life. They were right in the middle of every family plan or activity. In extreme cases a family might become "an autocracy capriciously and ineffectually ruled by its weakest member."

When a severely retarded child's condition became desperate or his behavior uncontrollable, then his family played out a losing game, a game that turned into a rout, and the very survival of the family was at stake. The unresolved crises and continued role disruption seriously strained family structure. These families in our study group were all intact at the time of the interview one to five years after commitment; but several individual members had been pushed beyond the limits of endurance, and temporary alteration of the household group through the hospitalization or departure of one spouse had occurred in several instances.

This has been a bleak description; yet there were positive elements in the situation that enabled most families to endure. That the parents continued to carry this burden of care so staunchly may be attributed in part to the peculiar role the retarded child acquired. He was in the family because he was "their own flesh and blood," but beyond that he acted to assert his claim to membership through relating to his family for affection and attention. Even the completely infirm child would assert such a claim, not just by being helpless but by receiving help and (some would assert) returning love:

> She never talked but you actually knew what she wanted. She made noises; there were delight noises and distress noises; we knew which was which. We could anticipate her needs; no one else could. I felt if only she could make her wants known to others—that's what bothered me.

This same child responded to her parents' efforts to walk her and seemed to delight in the voyages about the living room, supported by her braces and her father's hands.

The more capable children took an active share in family activites. Geoffrey C. worked happily and busily at little household tasks, rewarding his mother's efforts to train him. An older Italian gentleman enjoyed band concerts and ball games the more because his teenage boy and only son Joey had so happily responded. Most of the children could participate, some with enthusiasm, in the ritual of a family holiday meal or picnic. Very common was the mutual enjoyment of an automobile jaunt, with the retarded one seeming to respond with the excitement and pleasure of the young normal children.

Some of these children apparently possessed an aesthetic sensibility, an awareness of beauty. The mother of an autistic little boy felt this was so:

> He was a child who gave you nothing back, but you could feel sensitivity. . . . The things he could do have set him apart, like his love of music, his perceptiveness of beauty. He has delicacy and a dreamy way, if you could only get in to him. He has physical beauty. One of my friends said, "He's like a little fawn." You feel that there is a beautiful world there, if only you could get in and share it with him.

Some children sought to communicate this awareness. "I love the smell of the woods," confided a little boy who loved to wander there. A father and son enjoyed listening to records together; Natie C.'s rapt attention convinced his father that they shared a discriminating appreciation of Mozart and early Beethoven.

Parents remarked how children responded to their moods with sympathy, how they sometimes caught the child's mood. It might be a gay mood. Several of these children possessed a sunny nature and related happily and comfortably to their family. A few even shared family jokes, showed a sense of humor—parents were quite sure of this. Such a child would be encouraged to be an active participant in the family life. He would be a privileged actor, though; they would not hold him to the same standards they set for their normal children.

These elements of affect and interaction brought a soft focus to the picture the family had of their severely retarded child. (Rarely did they picture him in the harsh lineaments that the reality of this problem seemed to call for.) This picture the parents had influenced their hopes for keeping their retarded child at home and their expectations of what he could achieve there, and how in time he might develop under their care and training. These hopes were not extravagant, but usually they were based on the unrealistic assumptions that the family environment would somehow remain unchanged and the gap between the severely retarded child and his normal age-mates would grow no wider.

One wife recalled:

> When my husband and I had talked it over and accepted it a little bit, we said maybe someday an institution for her, but then we both put institution out of our minds. *We* would try first. We were doing well for her at home. Maybe when I had got her to sitting up well and maybe walking a little, then she might possibly —some specialized school but live at home. When I had thoughts of the future, she was always in it at home. And someplace along the line I just discarded completely the idea of an institution. The second child was real good and easy to take care of. But I got so I wasn't sleeping; I would lie there waiting for her convulsions, afraid I would not wake and there would be a serious one.

Her husband added:

> I never considered an institution, never did; thought she would always be with us. I could only conceive of her as being home all the time. The only thing that did trouble me was, "What will happen after we die?" Don't you think that was it (*turning to his wife*)? If she could only learn to ask for a glass of water, that is what we were shooting for.

This picture the parents had created for themselves. Their child's condition and behavior, the way he responded to them, and their own life experience and attitudes all entered into it. They clung to this idealized picture; they needed to see their child as a human personality, no matter how infirm or stigmatized he might be. When other people reacted to him as "just another sad case," the parents were distressed (the more so if their own lives had been harsh or insecure). Families would avoid exposing the child and themselves to a social situation where this was apt to occur.

Gradually, the hopes they had had for his future before discovery, or during those brief times since when "he showed flashes of the boy he might have been," were scaled down. Yet, even for realistic parents, there lingered aspirations for their child. This may have reflected their need for him to attain his maximum potential development. At any rate, all these parents still cherished goals for their retarded children, which varied with the ability of the particular child and the insight of his parents.

If their child was near the upper limit of the trainable, they might hope for him to become "independent, . . . learn to take care of himself in society"; or that he might receive further academic training, learn to read and write a little. For children at the median of the trainable level the wish was that the child might learn to talk more fluently, express himself more clearly, develop judgment that would enable him to avoid hazards and solve little problems. The hope was that in the future the child might be able to have some little job, something constructive, maybe "chores up at the farm."

When the retarded child's level of development was lower, parents had very modest goals. They wished that their child might learn to talk a little, to walk more steadily, walk at all, to express his wants and needs in some manner, to stand with assistance, and to move about, crawling. Lower still, they looked hopefully for some evidence that their child recognized them as his parents, if only by a smile or a look in his eyes. At the very lowest level parents had the goal that their child might be able to respond to affectionate comforting, play, and feeding, that he might be capable of emitting a little sound which to the attuned ear would convey pleasure or distress.

Chapter 3

The Family Problem of the Retarded Child

Severely retarded children always pose a manifold problem for their families. They involve their parents and siblings in a complex of adjustments and difficulties. This is the family problem of the child's retardation.

The parents in this study group did place an especial value on their severely retarded children and had given them assiduous care from their birth to their going away. The very survival of the children beyond early childhood attested to this care. But it had been to the increasing detriment of other family goals.

One family left their native state and kin—moved to another region a thousand miles away, where there might be help for their retarded daughter:

> We uprooted ourselves. We sold the house, furniture, and were on the train in two weeks. We made a quick decision. My relatives said, "Do not leave." But in the South you couldn't even whisper about it—something to be ashamed of. We packed up and left. If we had waited a month, the relatives might have persuaded us.

Other parents may not have taken such extreme measures, but in planning for their family they did put the retarded child's needs first.

Usually both parents continued interested in the severely retarded child, constructive in their efforts to help him and supportive of each other through the years from discovery to commitment and beyond. This was true even when a pair of parents had somewhat incongruent images of the retarded child, different definitions of the meaning of this problem for their family.

One mother who went alone to all the clinic consultations still felt she had her huband's agreement and support:

> He would always say, "You go." Then after the children had gone to bed, and the work was done, then we would discuss (in Polish) what happened with me that day at the clinic and what course of action should be taken. The children were never involved in any of this problem. We never discussed the decisions, medical or otherwise, with the children.

Strong mutual support was provided in the following case:

> [*Wife*] We took turns; I did most; my husband pitched in. Joyce started to take care of him early. She would watch him in the car when I went to the store.

In some cases the father was the reluctant one:

> [*Wife*] I felt very hurt when the neighbors said, "You are wasting all your years on this child. She should be in a home. You are young, and could be going out with your husband." Then my husband would come home and we'd fight. (How can I smile about it now?) He would say, "You're the mother and I'm the father and we've got to suffer. My kid isn't going anywhere." He's a better father than I am a mother! [*Husband*] She did the bulk of the work. I tried to help. I was away eight hours. She was home all the time. [*Wife*] Staying in the house didn't bother me.

Not always was there this mutual support. Cooperation sometimes faltered, and one parent took charge and tried to do it all alone. In reply to the probe—"Who took came of him—the mother?"—the answer was:

> And how! I was the only one to take care of Nicky. My husband had to work; I used to feel sorry for him. I'd say, "I'll do it, I'll do it!" until everything was piled up. Once in a while he'd hold Nicky for me so that I could get something done. . . .
>
> Myself, I became emotionally disturbed, for the simple reason I was overtired. I couldn't wait to place him. He was really out of hand, between the convulsions and the screaming. I couldn't take it any more. There was neighbors to consider, so I used to hold him all night so the neighbors and my other children wouldn't be disturbed. I would shut the windows so they wouldn't hear him. I was taking it all out on myself, trying to care for him. . . .
>
> I couldn't take it anyway. I would have left my husband and my children and everything else. I'm not cut out like that. You know I would have taken him down to the police station, with the way I felt at that particular time. I would say, "What do you want to do with me? I won't take care of the child anymore." I know I would have to go to the right authorities or somebody. I wouldn't be the type to kill it. I just can't do that. When I get like that I might as well be put away, too.

This mother of a large young family had become despairingly antagonistic toward the son she had come to regard as a menace to the very survival of her family. She finally persuaded her husband to apply for Southbury—he hadn't wanted his son "put away":

> Well, he didn't at first. It took me a while to break him in. It took me a while to adjust my husband. We talked it over and over, and finally when he saw his family and what it was doing to them and what we were going through, he saw it was the right thing to

> do but it took a while. I wanted to apply right after Dr. Samsel told us.

There probably were others who ultimately reached such extremity, but the majority of parents did handle their plight with the child as a mutual family problem right down to commitment. Personal suffering or disagreement over what to do with the retarded child had caused no permanent rift in any of these marriages. But it is certain that this experience affected the quality of the husband-wife relationship in every case. Even a couple who staunchly supported one another throughout could say:

> The whole family was high-strung all the way through. My wife and I—whatever we did it was always wrong. It was not that you were vexed at each other. It was the situation. The children cried easily. We couldn't talk to them or they'd start crying. . . . We'd get so physically exhausted, the lack of sleep and the hectic days; it was just a full-time job—and yet, we always had pretty good teamwork.

Coping with other internal family problems while the retarded child was still at home became increasingly difficult. One mother told of arrangements she had made for her new baby:

> We were really desperate, back against the wall. I made arrangements that if Marcia wasn't placed by the time the new baby was born, I would place the new baby in St. Anthony's Home.

Another mother, already pregnant, did not want to have another baby when she found out about the retarded one:

> That I didn't want! Ernie was on his way and I didn't want him. I just went to the doctors and started fighting them: "I don't want it! I don't want it!" I went to my regular doctor and to Dr. Michaels, may he rest in peace. They saw I was very upset. He promised me faithfully that if I had this child normally and well, they would have my tubes tied. . . . Now I could enjoy life. We don't have the worry and the strain on our heart that it's going to happen again. It's a big relief. I didn't want to spoil life for my other children.

It was clear from testimony of other parents that family fertility had been reduced by the presence of a severely retarded child in the home. Parents postponed having more children. There was a bigger age gap between the retarded child and his younger siblings:

> At first I was almost afraid. She was pretty close to three years old before I felt I really wanted to have another child; and then I had a miscarriage at three and one half months. So I was leery all over again. I had to go talk to my priest again.

After the discovery of the retardation most mothers had dreaded a subsequent pregnancy, even though reassured by their doctors or encouraged by their priest:

> I kept thinking, "Maybe it is something wrong with me, that I cannot bear a normal child." I did talk to the obstetrician and he was wonderful. If anybody drove a doctor out of his mind while carrying a baby, I was it. He was wonderful, listened to my nonsense, and had some real understanding. I had a different problem every time I went to see him.

Another mother recalled:

> I was afraid to have the second one, but not after that I wasn't afraid. I had wanted more. I talked to the visiting nurse. She was nice; I used to like the visiting nurses. She said, "Get another one and forget about the girl. All birds are not alike."

As it happened, in most of these families subsequent children had been born or conceived before discovery of the retardation. A couple volunteered:

> [*Wife*] The baby was born three weeks after we were told of Richie's retardation. I think it influenced me; I wouldn't go through another nine-month period of worry about it. . . . It was very fortunate to have Andy almost born; we wouldn't have had him otherwise. [*Husband*] What a loss that would have been! (*laughing*). You know, yesterday he walked in from school and called, "Hey, everybody, the King is home!"

Sometimes the advent of a next younger child was quite unexpected. The parents were especially grateful for these unanticipated additions:

> There was six years between Estelle and Frances, not because I was afraid, but because I had too much on my hands. I wanted to give all my time to Estelle. Frances was an accident, but we were glad to have her, and wished it had happened sooner.

In more than one case there was a later planned baby whose birth coincided with the ultimate commitment of the retarded child: "I got this one to take Lucia's place."

Any time there were other normal children it was better; the saddest cases in the study group were those few who had no other child. The new babies and their older normal siblings were an extra care ("I had to grow up like triplets! Three babies! The formula—oh my God!") They were also a great comfort. There was some future for them; they gave their parents something to plan for.

These families modified their everyday living patterns and sought to reorganize the home environment the better to cope with the problem.

Household roles, routines, and schedules were changed repeatedly to try to balance off the needs of the handicapped child against a minimal provision for the other members of the family. One mother even divided up the space:

> I had oilcloth on the porch floor. I used to wash it nice in the morning and put her out. We divided the porch in half, half for her and half for the other kids.

In extreme cases the safe custody and care of the retarded child took precedence over every other consideration in the organization of the home:

> I built fences all around the lot, micro-switches on the gates, a buzzer and bell hookup to the house, so that my wife could see whether he slipped out.

Another father said:

> This house was stripped to the essentials, a stove and a refrigerator, and she'd get on top of both of them. . . . One morning I came out in the kitchen. There she was sitting on the shelf of the stove, teetering back and forth letting her feet almost touch the hot stove top. She used to sit on that shelf; see how wobbly. That's something else I've got to fix around here. It's good to have the handle back on the refrigerator; we used to keep the handle up here, and the bolt that fastened it over in that drawer. Margaret would clean out the icebox!

A mother recalled:

> We all pitched in. My oldest son would watch her. He helped with the housework while I watched her. And my husband helped me a lot. . . . At two, the little one would take care of her; she would trot out and tell me when she thought Althea would get hurt, when she had something that could hurt her, or if she was climbing on a chair and might fall. . . . I had things to *try* to make things easy for me (*pointing to all the latest laundry equipment*) but sometimes I'd be washing at two or three o'clock in the morning!

There was corroboration from another mother who told of her routine:

> All day I used to be with the children—just change, feed and bathe them. Then at night I would do the hard things, wash the floor, do the washing, and then hang it up in the morning.

Another said:

> It wasn't just me; all the family took care of him. The father got up at five with him, would take care of him and play with him

until it was time to go to work. My boy couldn't take a job afternoons; all during high school he would come home and take care of Frankie for me. My boy's boy friends would take Frankie to the beach and watch out for him in the water. My daughter would come home from college every night to take care of him. He slept in with Jean.

The house was never clean like it used to be. I was lucky if I ever got the supper on.

Twelve years difference to Glenn, 15 years to Jean. They accepted responsibility. They never mentioned it, but it cut out their social life. . . . They loved him; they treated him as normal; they took him with them to their friends'. The thing that makes it the hardest is when you have other small children. My children were big; they were not ashamed of Frankie.

Though "it cut out their social life," well-established older brothers and sisters did bear the impact of this problem more sturdily than younger ones. Their socialization was more nearly complete. Their parents had had time for them when they were growing up.

If it was the eldest who was retarded, parents had more difficulty in socializing the younger children. Sometimes it was hard for them to act naturally toward their other children:

I think our whole life might have been different if Daniel had been normal. I think my husband would have been able to work more with the other children if he had been able to share the first child with me.

While discussing their retarded daughter's central role in the family, a set of parents described their contrasting relationships with their two young boys:

[*Wife*] John, the elder, had an easy-going nature, loving. He would crawl over to the sofa so as to kiss his sister. He had a long interest span; he would stay in his playpen or even right on the rug if I told him. It would take an hour to feed her. No problem—I used to pack the two of them in the station wagon. . . . Today he asked when he could go up to see her. . . . He is a very sympathetic child; he would hug her too hard; she would cry; then he would cry. At Southbury he runs to greet her. He realizes that she is sick, that that's her house up there, and that the nurses are helping her. He realizes that he would never have to go away like that.

If Jim, the younger, had come along first, I would have been out of my mind. . . . Two days before he was born, she went to Marlowe [a private hospital]. My husband and I were terribly upset all the time she was there. . . . A lot of Jim's trouble was my fault. . . . We placed her there temporarily; my husband's mother was no longer able to help. It lasted much longer than we thought. I was probably emotionally upset, and it influenced his babyhood. Looking back now, I probably made a lot of my own trouble. [*Husband*] John knows he is accepted here. For quite a while Jim fought us.

> . . . John was forever giving Martha something, doing something for her. Jim saw her as a rival for his mother's attention [even though she was never home after his birth].

Always the normal brothers and sisters were considerably involved in this problem. How deeply they were involved depended upon their own developing personalities, the behavior of the retarded child and their contact with him, and their perception of the behavior of their parents toward the defective one. The siblings early took on their parents' attitudes toward the retarded one. Parents imposed and the normal children generally accepted responsibilities beyond their age. Especially where the retarded child was the eldest would the next younger have to assume older-child roles. One family recalled:

> [*Husband*] When we had Estelle home, Frances was practically on her own. [*Wife*] I would say to Frances when she was one and a half, "Go get a diaper, a big one and a small one." Or she'd go to the store for me before she was two years old. She would feed Estelle. We took Estelle to St. Anne de Beaupre. Frances said, "St. Anne, we came up here. . . . You have to make my sister walk and talk."

Another couple spoke of their elder daughter's response toward her retarded brother:

> [*Wife*] She couldn't wait to get home from school each day. She was afraid she would find me upset! [*Husband*] She always did love him very much. [*Wife*] When I'd get mad, she'd take over and comfort him. [*Husband*] She had almost a mother instinct—never any feeling of resentment toward him. [*Wife*] She never mentioned the embarrassments Freddy caused her, so as not to worry me, I guess. [*Husband*] Away from home on a ride, we'd be pondering whether to stop and walk with him among strange people. She would always offer to take him. [*Wife*] My mother said she could manage him better than I could. [*Husband*] When he'd run away she'd race after him and grab him back. He was strong, but she still had a slight edge. There were three years and three months difference.

Parents of a twelve-year-old girl who was equally dedicated to her infirm older brother commented that she played in the house by herself most of the time, reading, drawing, watching television, since the retarded child had gone to Southbury. They discussed how she got along with other children:

> [*Wife*] Annette has grown up a lot more. She's not friendly with children. She'd say, "Susie is silly. She talks boys and plays records." Maybe it was growing up too fast. [*Husband*] We sent her to camp but she does not click. [*Wife*] A friend told me that it was not fair to Annette to have Charles home; it might spoil her chances. I told her that we wouldn't want anybody for her who

was that narrow-minded. When Charles was home, Annette would amuse him and help take care of him. . . . She was troubled what to tell the other children about Charles: "If I tell them he's three years old, they do not ask any more questions, but I do not like to lie. If I tell them he is fourteen, they keep asking questions. But they do not try to understand when I explain."

Even in the larger families, often just one particular child, close in age, assumed extraordinary responsibility toward the retarded one. Parents stressed that this child who had been their especial helper "grew up very fast," was warm-hearted, sensitive. This may have been an uneven growing-up, though. (One wonders about possible effects of such a sacrificing relationship, whether the surrogate mother role would help fit a child for the competitive teenage world.)

Other brothers and sisters, not so deeply involved, still participated actively in the family handling of the retarded child. If they were older than he, they could take care of him, "would watch him for a spell." If younger, they helped with the care, did little errands, and cooperating with the mother, "got independent." All the other children, so long as they were functioning within the boundaries of the home environment, or outside in the context of the retarded child problem, had to adapt their roles accordingly.

One mother tried unavailingly to protect her other children. She explained the early commitment:

> I wanted my other children to grow up normal, not to have anyone there to make them cry. . . . [When Nicky would have a convulsion] I would say to [five-year-old] Emily, "Stay out, stay out!" I didn't want her to see them. I kept her away. She never knew what it would look like. . . . Eileen was young enough to stay in the baby-tender most of the day. Ernie I had always in a crib; I'd wash him, change him, and put him away. Nicky would always be in the other crib or strapped on the bassinet. (The three of them—there is two years to the day—too close!)
>
> Emily used to play with her girl friends outside, but Eileen was right there. She saw Nicky's convulsions; and she say me crying all the time. And she and Nicky were so close of an age. . . . [*Husband*] Ernie is a different make. He is not affected. He is happy-go-lucky. He used to be leery of Nicky. [*Wife*] Eileen is the sensitive one. Definitely. She still worries about it constantly. She was old enough to understand well enough. That worry I cannot take away from her. . . . Lots of times Emily says that Eileen cries herself to sleep. She took in a lot and it does remain with her a long time.

In the following small family the retarded daughter was healthy and at the top of the sample in ability, and the parents were free to concentrate on both their girls. Yet there was increasing stress on the younger sister as the years went by:

[*Wife*] Clara used to push her sister a lot and pull her hair. Jeannette was getting to be a nervous child; she had that fear. She couldn't play or amuse herself like a normal little girl would want to. [*Husband*] Clara would break up her game.

[*Wife*] Say she wanted to play house—she'd set up something like cups and dishes, and they'd go flying. She'd say, "Oh, Mommy, I can't ever play." She used to wake up crying a lot nights. She was always on edge; she was always thin, couldn't put on weight. She used to demand my attention a lot; she used to cry a lot. She was jealous of Clara. I suppose she thought I was favoring Clara; I used to explain the best I could that that was the way she was. I used to try to let her go inside alone to work out a puzzle by herself.

She used to say, "Mommy, Clara is going to bother me now." They would start out nice to play; and then before you knew it, Clara would have eaten the crayons and Jeannette would go in to get her blanket, go into the corner and tickle her lip with it and suck her thumb. She still sucks her thumb; I didn't want to take it away from her completely. But she keeps herself busy, and it isn't as bad as it was. Just today, I explained to her that with a little baby coming it wouldn't be nice to suck her thumb. She tried to get along pretty well with her sister at Christmas. She still has that jealousy though.

She did most everything early, walked at nine months, and I found, myself, that after a while I expected too much of her. Because she could do things pretty well, I even used to blame her if something would go wrong. I would say, "Why don't you give it to her?" She'd feel bad when Clara would win all the time. It wasn't fair on the other child. I realized it after a while.

This kind of problem had an effect on the mental health of some of the other children. In three cases a sibling close in age to the retarded one had required psychiatric treatment. The oldest girl in a large young family was "treated at school for nerves." There may have been other such instances.

The physical health of siblings could be affected too. There were two cases of asthma in this study group, one so severe as to require a teenage boy to leave home and family and go alone to Arizona. (This boy did, however, have a history of severe experience with childhood diseases, including rheumatic fever.) His epileptic retarded sister at home had begun to have grand mal seizures at about this time.

The parents expressed a universal concern and showed the quandary that all these families faced:

[*Husband*] How do you know? This asthma—was there a psychological basis for it? Or what? We thought about that too. I don't doubt it did have an adverse effect on him. [*Wife*] You are bound to have to give more attention to the one who has the problems.

[*Husband*] You have two problems; you don't want to take away from the one who has a chance to have a normal life. From that viewpoint we probably should have tried to send her to Southbury earlier. If you could look ahead the way you can look back. . . .

Then there were allusions to school difficulties which had called for the therapeutic counseling of children. One case in particular stands out. A father looked back in retrospect at the relationship between his two sons:

From what we hear, it may have adversely affected Frank a little bit. Frank is very conservative; what Anthony did he didn't approve of always. He felt funny about Anthony. He asked, "Why do the kids make fun of Anthony? Why does he talk so funny? Why can't Anthony play with me?" Now he understands it much more.

Frank didn't like going to visit at Southbury, didn't like seeing Anthony at Southbury away from home. He would say, "Why should my brother be up there with all those funny-looking boys? There is nothing wrong with Anthony."

Frank went to kindergarten an extra year early, only so that my wife could devote time to Anthony. When Frank started kindergarten, Anthony wanted to go along too. He would sit there like a little gentleman, would thank the teacher if she served him crackers and milk. . . .

Frank? I don't know. There was a little competition for attention with Anthony. Company would always ask for Anthony, and Frank would lurk in the background. Anthony always got the little gifts from relatives and the neighborhood. A lot of people didn't know Anthony had a brother; Frank was just another little kid in the neighborhood.

Frank would make a big fuss over Anthony up at Southbury. He would give Anthony everything he owned. They loved one another but they didn't understand one another.

We now have an appointment with the psychiatrist from the Board of Education for Frank. For three years we have noticed this difference in Frank—daydreaming, lackadaisical. He's lost all his ambition. He'll start something, and then if it is a little too much for him, he quits. He takes everything for granted. He got a poor start with an older indifferent teacher. Each year he is not ready but they promote him. The teachers keep reassuring us. This year in fourth grade he has a good teacher who really is working on him. When I went to Florida on that brief visit, I took Frank with me and he did better after that.

This problem did affect school progress for all the young children. Even those reported bright did poorly in school during the years when the problem of the retarded child in the home was acute. These were important years in which reading and arithmetic skills need to be mastered. One couple remembered:

[*Husband*] Joyce did not have the carefree existence a child should have; although I do not think the responsibility hurt her. She was having trouble at school though—reading mostly. The teacher thought it was the pressure at home. [*Wife*] She was in third grade at the time. . . . She couldn't wait to get home from school each day. She was afraid she would find me upset.

One family was able to seek a remedy for the school problems early; the mother remembered:

When Dr. Hill went in and Dr. Tryon went out [at the Yale Child Study Center], they began to help as well as test; and we got Patty to going there when she went into third grade. She had been to nursery school, and in first and second grade she wasn't "reading, writing, and arithmetic." She was barely reading in the third grade; but when she left the third grade she was in the highest group.

Dr. Robinson thought the nursery school wasn't good and had her transferred to kindergarten. In the nursery school all the youngsters had to conform. Her kindergarten teacher said, "We aren't going to push Patty." They pretty much let her go her own gait. She was having temper tantrums in school. Richie's retardation affected her, no question about it.

We went to the Child Study Center for two years; she talked to one doctor and I talked to another. Then I used to bring her into school after the appointments. I never knew whether it was the good teachers she had in public school or the Child Study Center, but she picked up after that. Those good teachers understood her, helped her, let her go her own gait.

With the heavy demands of the retarded child, most mothers didn't have time to help their normal children work out the adjustments—school or social:

Frances had little or no care. When she started school I couldn't take her, and she came home and said, "All the other kids came with their mothers, and I was the only one." The afternoon PTA's I never could go to. The other kids could go home after it with their mothers. She'd have to wait until the regular closing time. She missed a lot.

Children might be adversely affected in their interaction out in the neighborhood. A sensitive little girl came home from school crying because the children teased her about her blind brother. A spunky little one stood up to the kids who called her sister a "dummy"; her mother described it:

She realized her sister's condition more than we did because the little children would remark about it to her. She felt that the other kids were always wrong. She'd say to them, "My sister can't help it if she can't walk or talk. Don't make fun of her. Someday you will be like that. God will punish you!"

While the retarded child was still at home the siblings' social life was limited. They couldn't have other children in to play, or entertain with birthday parties during the severe phase of the problem. One mother explained:

> He told everybody about his retarded sister. He's very proud of her, even though she is a sick girl. The only thing, he never could have boys in. He was deprived of that, but he never complained. He would understand that maybe the other boys might resent her.

Even where things weren't critical at home, the picture was similar:

> I used to find that Jeannette would want to play with some little girl and ask her over, but because Clara was there the little girl would make an excuse to go off. If she knew Jeannette was alone, she'd be more than willing to play with Jeannette.

Sometimes a hostile neighborhood further limited the siblings' social life. One couple were sure of this:

> [*Husband*] We got booted around some. We were in like a project, close together. With birthday parties, they wouldn't invite our children. It was the parents more than the children. [*Wife*] The neighbors' attitude was a contributing factor and our other children suffered. . . . There were a few kindly neighbors. But the neighbors weren't too kindly; they used to keep their kids away.
>
> [*Husband*] The time Sheila came home covered from head to foot with tar—the Moisio kids threw this creosote, roofing tar at her. We told their mother and she said, "So what!" She wouldn't want to know what they did. They blamed Sheila for everything. Those kids didn't turn out so hot either. [*Wife*] Sheila would just stand there and let them do things like that.

This father continued: "It would have been rather rough if she had stayed at home. I thought of getting a big place and fencing it in." But his wife demurred, "Then you're fencing in your other children, and fencing me in too. I have enough of that on rainy days now."

Sometimes the neighborhood provided a favorable environment which tactful outgoing parents could build on in fostering the social adjustment of all their children, including the retarded one:

> [*Husband*] But it is country living; all three homes [in the neighborhood] have been open to the kids. It's been like one family; all three homes were like one home. . . . [*Wife*] All the children come in here for cookies. We had the playground, the soda machine, the ice cream cones. I was always at the kitchen door. And this was a pretty nice place to hang around for the kids. There wasn't the refreshment at the other homes. . . .
>
> But we did not take an overprotective attitude toward Richie. We could have taken the protective attitude and could have kept him and our other kids away.

This retarded child was a friendly little boy, socially acceptable; and the neighbors felt warm toward him. When a retarded child was infirm or hyperactive or stigmatized the best practice was for parents to seek a limited participation in the life of the neighborhood for the sake of their normal children, while trying to suppress the harsher aspects of this problem and contain the retarded child at home.

Chapter 4

Family Relationships—Interaction with Others

Those parents were fortunate who during the long course of this problem could rely on the continuing help and counsel of their family doctor or pediatrician, because the health problems of all the members of these families were extraordinary: There was the question of whether to have more children; that was one concern these parents shared with their doctors. Also, they and the other children were especially vulnerable to illnesses; they required preventive care and frequent medical attention. In the last years of the child's stay at home tuberculosis might threaten the mother; necessary operations were postponed; the father might become emotionally upset; another pregnancy might occur; and it was the ministrations of the doctor that kept the family going.

As for the retarded ones—even a strong and healthy child posed difficulties for medical treatment (he fought taking medicine), while an infirm child required constant attendance by the pediatrician (infections and minor children's diseases were catastrophes for him).

The mother of a large young family exclaimed:

> Dr. Naylor lived at our house! . . . I think Dr. Naylor was my faith and my helping hand. . . . It was Dr. Naylor who took care of him and gave us the support. He didn't try to pass his own opinions. We talked over all those reports with Dr. Naylor. How many times he didn't take for the visit when we had all the children with colds! His heart bled for us. I probably wouldn't have placed Nicky so early if it wasn't for Dr. Naylor. My conscience was clear; he is a doctor who knows all the medical terms.

When parents had this confident access to a supportive professional, they were better able to carry out recommendations for the care and management of the retarded child and resist the strains on their family life.

For the majority of families not so fortunate, even a fortuitous contact with a perceptive, sympathetic doctor could be a real help at a critical time. A wife who had been troubled over the commitment decision recalled:

> My husband had charge of the fruit department at North Hills Market. Dr. Nelson Strong talked with him about Todd. When he heard what I had done, he said I had done all right with Todd at home, everything right, and that now it was a question of waiting. . . . The Cerebral Palsy clinic had spoken of Southbury. . . . Dr. Strong told me a little about it, that they could help him, that they would give him a trade and might do him good; but then he turned around and said, "You're the mother of the child. You know what is best for him. Do what you think is best." Dr. Strong had a lot to do with it.

To some parents, however, even the best pediatricians or general practitioners appeared disinterested, clinical, not at all supportive. Their impersonal pessimism discouraged the parents. Other doctors were conscientious, sympathetic, but indecisive or inept in their early communication with the parents.

One popular pediatrician avoided any mention of the mental retardation, thinking it better for mothers to gradually discover it for themselves. He was glad to serve the children's medical needs, but he didn't want the problem of mental retardation to intrude. Unintentionally, he lulled one set of parents into false hopes, making it hard for them to accept other doctors' more forthright counsel.

Some pediatricians were reluctant at belatedly assuming such a case, even with an influential reference:

> He was very nice to us, but gruff: "What do you expect of me bringing me a child like this, especially when you bring him when he is three months old?"

A few pediatricians probably did not want these retarded children for patients at all, and perhaps intentionally antagonized the parents at the first office visit. One mother recalled bitterly:

> This doctor said, "Your little boy will never walk, talk, or know anything. Now, what shall we do about it?" I put my baby in the blanket and went out that door crying like a maniac.

One doctor, who had had the care of the children in a family for some time, including the retarded one, became evasive, according to the mother's testimony: "I find nothing wrong with the child, but I will make an appointment at the New Haven Hospital pediatric clinic." When this family persisted in calling him he would consistently refer their calls to other doctors.

This same family did make early application, but in the intervening four years went to a number of doctors and voluntary agencies. Occasionally one would raise false hopes, would urge them to hold off a while on Southbury. Fortunately, this road finally led them to the Crippled Children's Association, where the consulting doctor helped the mother to understand:

> There was nothing that would help him. He might be taught to sit up and be toilet trained, but nothing else. And he just told me to bring Jerry to the clinic for massages, and just wait for our Southbury application. He told me point-blank: "Do not spend your money. This child cannot be helped, except as Southbury can do it." . . . [She was grateful;] And yet it took our little hopes and put it straight that that was the end of it. The others had all promised that there might be something.

Occasionally doctors consulted parents:

> When Anthony got to be about six years old, Dr. DeLeito would call me and ask, "What do you do when Anthony does this?" He was quite frank that he was seeking the advice to help another mother with the same problem. Other mothers used to call up and inquire what to do with different ailments. Anthony had had them all.

Once a pediatrician asked a mother to talk with a young couple who had a newborn mongoloid baby:

> They came over to advise with me. I put Daniel in his running pants so they would feel free to look at him; I went upstairs, so they could stare at him all they wanted to. Then I told them it was their own decision. I said that in my particular case I enjoyed and loved him, and it was the best thing for me personally, and that Daniel was no particular problem to me personally to keep at home. They were young, only 25 years old. I thought it could help them to make up their minds whether to place him or not. . . . I thought it was nice of Dr. Robinson to think of this; I would have appreciated something similar myself.

Some families spent considerable money for experimental treatments or a continued round of medical consultations, "to Boston and New York . . . to a lot of other doctors in the meantime"—this in spite of the fact that right at home there were excellent medical facilities.

Several purchased new homes with a hope for the child's better adjustment in a sheltered environment. There was always a marked change in the pattern of family spending. When the retarded child was hyperactive, there might be no new party dresses, just new dungarees for mother and retarded daughter; no vacation trips for the family, just a dependable car to take the child riding. When the child was physically disabled and infirm, orthopedic appliances and medical treatment might entail heavy expenses. A father remarked:

> We'd have a house by now. . . . I make enough. . . . I bought a suit this year, the first in eight years. . . . Today maybe she could spend three dollars for a dress!

The most onerous financial burden of all was the cost of a desperate emergency placement of a retarded child in an inferior private facility:

> [*Wife*] The Marlowe year was the worst and he was working nights and Saturdays to pay for it. . . . [*Husband*] I took my vacation and went to work for a contractor.

Often, expenses attributable to the retarded child caused the father to strain to increase his income. For a semiskilled worker this meant a second job or longer hours. One such father, an older man, said:

> We have had to pay out anywhere from $1,200 to $1,500 a year for schools, plus expenses to visit him. . . . We bought a car to go to see Alfred. We had to work a lot more. I have put in fifty or sixty hours a week. My wife has been back working.*

Another couple were rueful:

> [*Wife*] I wish I had the money I spent on that boy! We were never able to put a dollar away. [*Husband*] It has kept us pretty well drained ever since he was born. Those big profit-sharing checks that we used to get at the end of the year during the war were so opportune. [*Wife*] The first year I had Anthony it cost $500 and we didn't have it. The following year I went in for another operation, another big bill.
>
> [*Husband*] We didn't have any habits of spending. We got married on a shoestring. We probably would have had a home. I would not have been working where I am today; I would have gone to school some more.
>
> I stayed with the same firm; I grew up with the company. I started as receiving clerk and worked up, but could not go to school for advanced training. I almost started a little business of my own. I did take a correspondence course in electronics.

Always this problem had a sharp effect upon a father in his breadwinner role. In understanding this effect it helps to distinguish between task behavior and performance behavior—getting the job done and getting along on the job. Both aspects are evident in the following:

> [*Husband*] I don't want to be Pollyannic about it, but it induced me in some stages to do better work. I had to get more money. The year she was critical I advanced three grades, which was very unusual. My personality at work probably was not the best. [*Wife*] It wasn't; he had very little sympathy for anybody else. [*Husband*] I wasn't running in a popularity contest! I chewed out the workers. My troubles were bigger than theirs. But they thought *they* had problems—a tough hangover, somebody sick at home, they didn't

* At the time of the interview this man near sixty was at home disabled from an industrial accident—he had been "pulled over the rollers." Apparently recovering, he died two years later, the first of the parents to die.

like the coffee where we stopped for a break. Today I am much easier to get along with at work; we get through the day somehow.

It may have been harder for fathers who had to supervise workers or deal with the public as managers when this problem at home was acute. One father sadly described the effect on his career:

> My wife would plead with me, "Could you take a day off? I had such a bad day with Andrew yesterday. I have a headache this morning." Quite soon I saw myself taking too many days off, and I lost out on quite a few opportunities for promotion.
>
> I just had one-half the amount of patience that I should have had with the public. My disposition wasn't any too good. Most of the time my mind was at home wondering what Andrew was doing, how my wife was holding out, watching the clock until I could get home to relieve my wife. I had much difficulty in concentrating on my work.

Only rarely did a father handle both aspects of his work life successfully during the course of this problem. One replied as follows to the question, "Did it have any effect on you at your work?":

> In times of great stress it might have, but not for long. I am the kind of person that gets fully absorbed in one thing. When I come home from work for the weekend, I forget where I work, and vice versa. . . . I went from the factory to research at the time he was born. I worked on up.

Such fathers who could find an outlet and satisfaction in their work, who were in touch with home but not preoccupied, were also very supportive of their wives and other children.

Most fathers muddled through at work, their load sometimes eased by a tolerant employer or sympathetic fellow workers. A steelworker contributed:

> I would go to work worried, because I knew my wife would have a hard time, and I wished I could be home to help her. The fellows were all nice to me because they knew I had a sick child on my hands.

The work environment wasn't always sympathetic and some fathers just didn't elicit sympathy:

> It didn't affect my work. I always had plenty to do. I never discussed it with anyone at work; I just discussed it with those two doctors, but not with a lot of people. To hell with them; it's none of their affair! So-and-so tries to needle me; he says, "What year is she in high school?"

With the neighbors there had to be some communication about this problem of the retarded child; the neighbors were close at hand. Families varied widely in how they handled this communication. Just a few parents were quite comfortable with neighbors, talking about it with them, relating to the neighbors' young children, bringing out in plain view their retarded child, readily accepting the neighbors' help but effectively keeping him from being a burden on the neighborhood:

> [*Wife*] We had a fenced-in yard, but he would climb the fence. My sister was horrified because I tied a long clothes line rope around his waist with the other end tied to a post. He had the whole freedom of the yard, and he could remain out when I had to be inside with the babies. The neighbors were wonderful; the policeman and his wife would move the rope and tie it to their porch so that he could be in the shade. Earlier my husband had built a fence, but Daniel would knock the slats out. My sisters thought we were treating him like a dog, but they never helped any. I knew we were doing the right thing. And as long as you have to make the big decisions yourself, people ought to leave the little ones for you to decide. . . . I have wonderful neighbors. A next door neighbor was very sympathetic; he spent hours trying to teach Daniel to walk. He used to tie a sling from a necktie and put it under his arms and hold him up. He would stand Daniel up against a wall, and have me hold my arms out and call him. I used to cry and tell him to leave him alone. I was afraid he'd fall and get hurt. Boy, did I cry that day he walked! That was real excitement. [*Husband*] It took quite a few weeks.
>
> [*Wife*] The only unhappy incident—there were two little boys who used to hang over the fence. They'd say, "That kid is nuts." They'd take his toys out of his reach to tease him. I came out with fire in my eyes to chase them. But then I changed my mind and decided to talk to them instead of punishing. I said, "I want to tell you boys something. God didn't make him like He made you; that little boy can never go to school, or play games with other children or have friends. Now because God gave you the ability to have those things, you should feel sorry for him." Their heads were down. I said, "I want you to think about it." I never had any more trouble with them; I don't think they came through this way anyway again.
>
> I kept Daniel in his playpen or tied to the long rope or in the fenced-in yard. The little neighbor girls loved to come over; they'd compete to feed him; we'd make cookies. I went to each mother when we moved here and explained about Daniel and asked them would they explain to their children, would they tell me if he ever got loose, for it would be by accident. If the door was open he'd scoot across the street. Some people try to hide it and lie about it, keep it covered up. I don't think we ever had that problem of misunderstanding. The trouble comes when people do not understand.

The mother and father of a delicate, pretty, crippled child described neighborhood contacts:

[*Wife*] If they asked me any questions, I explained it as fully as I could. [*Husband*] A new family—one of the kids banged her with a gun. We explained to the father how she was handicapped—"We leave her out; we do not feel that we have to take her in the house because you have moved into the neighborhood. So you explain to your child." The father did talk to him. Andy never caused any more trouble after that. [*Wife*] Once we moved here, I felt more relaxed about it. I was so thrilled that she could be out all day, even when it was hot and sunny. We bought her a beach umbrella. [*Husband*] It was an education process. We had to tell everyone. She was outside all day. . . . [*Wife*] I was amazed, they accepted her so completely. She was out in front every day; the kids would play around her; then come up and say, "Are you all right, Martha Ann?" Only once a kid sprinkled her with the hose; his mother, a friend, was in tears about it. (Before, when we lived in that low-rent housing development, it was real tough over there. I couldn't leave her outside alone.) With her braces on I'd be exercising her, and they'd be in on it, "Oh, look, Martha Ann is walking!" or I'd be pushing her in the stroller, and they would want to walk along with her.

One family with a healthy, handsome, hyperactive nine-year-old boy was very open about this problem. They credited this openness for the understanding and help they received:

[*Wife*] Speaking out about it! Explaining his handicap, what it was. It's something to live with. Everybody has accepted it. We've never hidden it. [*Husband*] Sure, keep it out in the open. [*Wife*] We never have been ashamed of it. . . . [*Husband*] The kids next door would play "Freddy," the way he'd run around and wave his arms and climb. Our Judy would play right along with them. He was accepted in the neighborhood. Everyone was sympathetic. . . . All the neighbors were good. Why, the man next door, they didn't have any children then, would come over and play with him. Another neighbor was taking a nap. His wife saw Freddy go over the fence. She woke him. He went after him in his stocking feet. They were all on the alert. They would just go chasing after him and bring him back.

An older couple, long established in their home, contributed:

[*Wife*] The children, of course they'd laugh. It was only the children. [*Husband*] The neighbors were very good. [*Wife*] I didn't say anything harsh to the children; the little fellows didn't understand. Joey would say something and they would laugh. And I'd say, "Play nice together." In fact, all the neighbors wanted to punish their children on account of Joey but I said they shouldn't—"They do not understand; they are just little children." [*Husband*] We had good neighbors. [*Wife*] He hardly wanted to stay out. He wanted to stay with me. I had to be with him. I would say to him, "Go

> downstairs; watch the children play on the swing." The neighbors would say to their children, "Give Joey the swing." I had nice ways with the children; I'd say, "I'll swing you and then you." [*Husband*] As he got older, he wouldn't move away from us. . . .
>
> [*Wife*] As to talking about it, I didn't find it uncomfortable; only we didn't say much to the neighbors; maybe they wouldn't want to listen to our story. . . . Oh, I felt bad and my friends felt bad. Everybody said, "Oh, such a lovely couple." It was hard.

A modern couple in a city apartment house occupied by young professional people described their social life with neighbors:

> [*Wife*] When we lived on Howe Street, she was always known as a sick baby. When we moved here, at two years old she was better physically. The level of intelligence is high in this building. I explained to all the neighbors as I met them. She was warmly received. She became a pet around here. She was sunny and pleasant. [*Husband*] I can't think of any unpleasantness we had with the neighbors. It was no problem at all explaining. We found people were very sympathetic and didn't treat us as though we were monsters. The only instance I can recall was my wife's girl friend was pregnant. She is not an intellectual powerhouse. [*Wife*] She didn't want to wear some maternity clothes that I had, superstitious that it might be catching. They all liked Ruth. They all came up and visited with us and were very pleasant when we took her to Southbury.
>
> [*Husband*] Our apartment is always the center of activity. They look to my wife, "What shall we do today?" My wife is the person who the others would look to for ideas. [*Wife*] They loved her. [*Husband*] They treated her well. I mentioned before, many retarded children you do not want to look at them. Their facial expression might hurt you. Ruth, except for her eyes, was a very pleasant child. Her eyes didn't focus on anything; they wandered away. I imagine if she had not been so pleasant to look at, some of them might have shied away.

Perceptive, sympathetic neighbors who met the parents with their retarded child more than halfway, who were warmly disposed toward the child yet casual in their treatment of him, were indeed a boon. Yet some parents just could not relate to their neighbors. A lonely couple who had lost their first child and whose second child was retarded moved with him to a good neighborhood, where people were not unkind. But they felt:

> [*Husband*] There was no sense talking with neighbors. They are not interested. [*Wife*] I haven't any friends. Nobody wants to know anything about that. [*Husband*] They are not interested. What can they do? [*Wife*] You're shunned. I'm beginning to say I haven't a child. It would be better for us if we got in with other parents with a similar problem.

> [*Husband*] The neighbors' kids get frightened, why I do not know. He isn't a vicious child. . . . The crippled ones have two strikes on them before they even start. . . . The children will not associate with him. It's senseless, the children will not play with him. [*Wife*] After we knew about it, we kept him by himself. I'd call him over and I wouldn't let him. . . . We didn't let him go where other people are. I was too sensitive. Next door—she used to come over all the time. She liked Alfred, but she talked about her own boy too much. I ignored it. I had to have someone to talk to. I talked to everybody to some extent.

Some parents withdrew from relatives and former friends. Said a wife:

> I stayed a little more in the park by myself, but I had always been the jolly type. I changed from one extreme to another. Rarely did we get a call from our friends any more. . . . I tried to avoid anybody who had children. There would be hard feelings. They try to be polite. We've developed a terrible attitude toward people.

On the other hand, only in deteriorated, unstable neighborhoods did families experience any grievous trouble with their neighbors:

> Last year Estelle was outside on the back porch in her stroller. Thump thump I heard. I went out to check. On the floor of the porch I find all rotten fruit, and garbage all over the floor. This kid was throwing it up on the porch. I cried—"I want to get out of here. Someone might disfigure her."

Having a friend who would take some share in the problem was very important to these parents. For a father this might be a good friend with whom he could talk freely when he needed to, or could just find companionship:

> I asked a couple of my husband's friends to take him somewhere, a baseball game, to shoot pool, anywhere, so he'd relax. He never went out. If he got out and relaxed, maybe he would talk about it to them; he wouldn't to me.

The father of a severely and profoundly retarded child warmly remembered a good friend who relieved the family's isolation and gave them a little lift:

> We used to take Althea to one friend's house. He had a great thick engineering book that she used to love to rifle over. My friend would hand her the book and say, "What phase of engineering are we going to take up tonight?" She would sit happily in a chair with that book. Then when we got ready to take her home, he would ask, "Well, what did you learn tonight?"

For a mother it was important to have a close friend, a confidante. One mother described such a relationship:

A girl friend of mine who used to be a nurse at the Masonic Home, she gave us a lot of moral support. . . . She has a part-of-the-family feeling for Freddy, and she has three youngsters of her own. . . . For years we couldn't visit people in their homes with our children, except the Johnsons' and my mother's.

Sometimes a relative would fill this role. One mother told of her younger sister, devoted to her and to her retarded daughter:

My sister would take Carlotta out more than I would—on the bus, to see Santa Claus, even to the movies. Carlotta would stay quietly with her at the movies. She took her to the show to see *Cinderella*. . . . When my sister was around, I could not do anything for Carlotta—"No, Auntie Dolly does it"—wash her, dress her, fix her hair.

The lack of a close friend or the loss of an intimate relationship at this time really hurt:

Wesley came between a good friend and me. . . . There was one particular friend who didn't understand. She had looked to me to do things. She was more or less jealous of Wesley. She looked to me to baby her. She asked my son's friend about Wesley; then she said some awful things he would never repeat. He wouldn't tell my son what they were. . . . I didn't feel I had *anybody* I could really talk to. I wanted somebody to talk to, but there wasn't anybody. I wasn't close to my mother. There wasn't even a minister's wife that I could go to who would help me. That first year I just felt, if I only had *somebody* to talk to.

Early at discovery time it was important to have a close friend to talk to. During the years the retarded child remained at home and throughout the commitment stage such a friendship was invaluable; it helped keep mother and father from becoming isolated with the problem. Sometimes it was friends rather than doctors who were most supportive in the commitment process, who effectively guided parents to a decision for placement. Such a friend is speaking here:

This old friend of mine came up to me one day. I hadn't seen him for a long time. And he said, "You know, Bill, I have a child like yours." And I said, "Southbury is such a wonderful place. Bring your wife over to our house to meet my wife." We got them to apply for Southbury for their little one. We said, "Take a ride with us and take a look at my daughter and the school." We became very good friends.

The couple receiving this friendly help had been very unfortunate in their relations with doctors.*

* The response by the couple receiving the help is given in Section I, Chapter 6, "Waiting for a Place at Southbury."

In a few cases it was neither a doctor nor a friend, but a social caseworker who helped a family most through the crisis period. This caseworker may have come to fill the role of family confidante:

> [*Wife*] Miss English, a social worker of the Crippled Children's Association. . . . She told me about Southbury. She listened to my problems. She never came out and said we should do it, but she assured me that Martha would get good care. . . . I talked with Miss English, who got me the form . . . a tremendous wonderful person. She would just come by for a cup of tea, and without your realizing she would help so much. To this day I consider her my dear friend. [*Husband*] She had the coolest head of any.

Even when parents felt free to talk about this problem and seek or accept help from friends and neighbors, interpreting their child's deficiency to their own extended family was difficult. Getting the relatives to understand this problem required patience and tact. A grandfather, very active and concerned with this problem, woud not be reconciled to the finality of it:

> [*Wife*] It was just terribly hard for him to accept. [*Husband*] Father did not take it for final. [*Wife*] After every one of his junkets, he would come bouncing out to see us, and ask hopefully, "Now how is Arthur?" as if almost he had expected a transformation had taken place during his absence. It was so hard to tell him that Arthur was just about the same.

Another wife corroborated this family pattern of supportive concern yet lack of acceptance:

> My folks loved her; it was hard to convince them there was anything wrong; she was the only granddaughter. They thought a lot of her, my folks did—not exactly as a normal child [later on], but they were happy to see her.

Sometimes the parents had to do the comforting:

> My mother took this very hard—her first and only grandchild. It had looked for a long time as though there never would be any. I spent a great deal of my energy pacifying her, instead of weeping over it myself. It may have been better that way.

Collectively, the wider family, even though sympathetic, could not really share:

> Here you are, your oldest retarded. You go to see your mother. The other brothers and sisters have children, nothing wrong with them. They all look and shake their heads. Then you don't go.

Often, the wider family could not identify with the retarded child. Even in an old-world family there was not this much solidarity. A couple tried to convey this:

> [*Wife*] The younger ones, our age, who had children just didn't understand, did not try to much; but they would give advice—"I shouldn't send him around the streets; I got a lot of nerve!" [*Husband*] After Anthony got to be about four or five we kind of broke away from our friends with young children. He couldn't compete; he'd get hurt easily. He'd cry, "Why can't I play ball like the other boys do? Why I always sick?" Even with the in-laws about our age that had children about the same time that we had Anthony—their kids made such progress. There were four nieces and nephews all born within a couple months; it would hurt seeing these other children running around and doing things that Anthony couldn't. They would all come over to visit Grandma; we lived with Grandma. Then the other children would get a little afraid of Anthony as his voice changed on account of the croup. But all this got better as Anthony got older, for everyone loved Anthony.

Infrequently, even close relatives weren't sympathetic; they might be hostile. When a nuclear family experienced a barrier to understanding, suffered from criticism of their handling of the retarded child, or felt that relatives' help was grudging, then a rift would develop:

> My relatives were giving us that kind of advice—"The child is spoiled; there isn't any discipline; you are too lenient. If you clamp down on him, he will improve. There is nothing wrong with him that a whipping won't cure. (They had been told but they wouldn't accept it.) The child might be a little slow, but the right upbringing and he would behave okay." All this didn't do my wife any good at all.

In another case it was:

> My mother didn't want to have any part of it. She probably considered it a stigma to herself. I think my mother never discussed it. My mother gave Christmas presents one year to the other two boys, but not to Daniel. That bothered me—the deliberate slight—that he wasn't in the family. I'll never forget that; I felt so bad. I never told anyone at the time; but later I told my dad or my sister and the next year there was a present for Daniel too. That attitude of my mother's was the hardest thing I had to put up with. They would never inquire how Daniel is since he went to Southbury. I cannot understand it. Maybe she feels a guilt complex.

These were extreme cases. Usually, a negative phase with the relatives came early, when the parents themselves were having a hard time adjusting; and it didn't last long. Things would get better with the relatives as they had a chance to observe the child's behavior and learn more about his problem. More common was the following assessment of behavior toward a retarded child:

> [*Husband*] With the relatives there was a little mixture, I guess. Not in a hard way, I guess. [*Wife*] When it was her birthday, they

all came up and gave her a gift. They respected her there. They all liked her, were nice to her; they didn't show any dislike to her. [*Husband*] A mixture like they didn't want to take care of her, but they didn't feel hard toward her.

Apart from their attitudes toward the retarded child, the relatives were usually concerned for the family. If they couldn't help with the retarded child, they would take care of the siblings; and some individual relatives did give assistance with the retarded one:

My younger sister would always come and sit with Freddy if we asked her.

Once your sister-in-law took Margaret, that same sister-in-law [who once had Margaret for four months]. She was the only one that knew Margaret. Anybody else, we had to tell them too much. . . . Just when I went to the hospital for the baby she took Margaret for two weeks. She was wonderful, she still is.

Ellen, my sister, had a friend with a retarded child. She was very understanding. . . . We'd often have Elizabeth with my folks if we wanted to go anywhere. My wife's sister would help that way too.

My mother has a lot of patience with her. She'd talk to her and manage.

They helped as best they could; my brother, my mother would come. The only one I could really talk to was my brother. . . . He's more talkative [sic] than anybody. "The old lady," my husband calls him. He is the one who used to drive me to New Haven Hospital all the time because he was available in the day.

Furthermore, there were a few couples who stressed the empathy their families showed all the way through. One mother was very sure of her relatives' love and warmth for her infirm daughter:

When they came to visit, they showed her a lot of affection; she was so pretty, lovable, and happy. I cannot think of any one of them that thought of her simply as a sad case; I think she was felt to be an individual to them. We were very fortunate in our choice of relatives.

Another couple gave this illustration of support and love from their family. They recalled a big Thanksgiving reunion to which they had journeyed with their retarded boy. When they brought him to the table for the holiday dinner he had a tantrum, upset by the excitement and the crowd. The whole family waited quietly and unobtrusively until he settled down then they joined them, and they started dinner.

An older couple felt they had understanding from their families:

[*Wife*] My mother and my niece treated him so good. They had lots of patience with him. My mother would say, "After all he is

> like that." He wanted to win all the time. Everybody was very nice to him. In both families, everybody was very nice to him. I used to take him to my family. My sisters were all very nice to him. There are nine living now in my family; I am the oldest. [*Husband*] They gave him all his way. [*Wife*] The only place I used to take him was to relatives; friends you know, you'd feel bad—you don't know how they will react. Everybody was so nice to him; that's one thing that would make you feel good, you know. He wasn't the kind, though, that would break things.

A grandmother, a recent widow, was very supportive in the care of the child; this was a solid family and she and her late husband had been an integral part of it. It was she who answered: "*We* did not have any trouble with the close relatives; *they* did not interfere." Ultimately, it was this grandmother who took a leading role in placing the child at Southbury. Yet she did not relish this role: "It is a very hard thing to do. If the earth covers it up, at least you know no one is abusing it." But she also firmly felt: "That one child would have ruined every one else's life around here, those two young boys!"*

* This elderly Jewish grandmother lived in the flat downstairs. Before the interview started, she telephoned, "Can I come up?" Interested in the study and quickly reassured by the explanation, it was she who suggested, "Let's all sit around the dining room table!" Most of the evening she kept a tight rein, occasionally answering *sotto voce* questions directed to the retarded child's mother. Her several contributions were cogent.

Chapter 5

Family Activity—Community and Associations

Most families knew they shouldn't stay at home in isolation with their retarded child, so they tried to conserve their relationships. In the early stages most families kept up some social activity too, worked out adaptations that let them carry on in a limited way. But inevitably their circle of acquaintances diminished, and their contacts with close relatives and intimate friends changed selectively:

> You really couldn't entertain; you didn't know what she was going to do. You couldn't go out; she wasn't the type of child you could get a babysitter for.

A mother recalled:

> I tried to stay in my own yard, my own house, my car. I wouldn't go visiting. People who didn't have a child in the family like that couldn't understand. . . . We just dropped everything. . . . I got out of touch with all my girl friends. I had a ladies' club; I dropped out of that. I used to get together with the girls and go to a movie and I dropped out of that too.

Sensitive herself anyway, and preoccupied with the care of two difficult children, one unpredictable and the other "nervous," this mother just gave up all social life and withdrew into her immediate family. Her own parents were helpful. Her husband was especially understanding and supportive. More gregarious than his wife, nevertheless he also automatically dropped out; "baseball, handball, getting together with the boys once or twice a week—or go out and you know—I just dropped out completely."

For a couple who had moved a thousand miles in order to place their brain-damaged child at Southbury, the waiting period was indeed a withdrawal time:

> [*Wife*] it made no difference while we were still in Benning. [*Husband*] We would still visit around down South. We came to Connecticut and had no friends for quite a while. Friends we made later said that my wife went around with a chip on her shoulder. [*Wife*] I did a lot of things wrong. She looks normal, but to take her out

in public was just too much for me. I could not stand the stares. I would just stay home. . . . When we first came north I discouraged all the neighbors' efforts to be friendly.

There was this tendency for all families to retreat with the retarded child into their home circle. One can sympathize with the ones who in their sadness sought seclusion. Said one mother:

I always found it hard then; I would try to hide it. I didn't want to talk to people at all. I felt so bad. . . . When you have one like our own, you turn your head not to stare at one on crutches or disfigured. . . . I didn't want to be bothering anyone with him. I couldn't be taking him to the neighbors' homes.

Another, the mother of a hopelessly ill child, said:

I had been very active at the PTA's, and the minute it happened to the baby I couldn't go anymore, because I couldn't discuss it. The minute anyone asked me about the baby I'd just start to cry. I wasn't ashamed of it, but when I'd tell them they would feel so badly about it. That would make me feel worse.

It wasn't just parents' sadness and sensitivity that caused this withdrawal from social life; it was more the status of the child, the effect of his behavior or the extent of his impairment. Her young son's abysmal condition and disruptive behavior ruled out all social activity for one mother:

Yes, it did, definitely. I kept away from everyone; I didn't go out. I just felt bad I had that type of child. [*Husband*] If he took a convulsion when we were out! [*Wife*] But I didn't want them to see him take a convulsion; I didn't want them to come into the house. I felt it was our burden. I wasn't mad at the world, that they should have one too, but I just didn't want them to see him with the convulsions. . . . How could anyone else understand? It's best alone. No one has anything to say. What good is pity?

When an infirm child slowly deteriorated over a span of fourteen years at home, this had to have an enduring effect on the parents' behavior:

[*Wife*] I've changed. I used to be good-natured. Now I get huffy about any problem, the way the colored people are treated or anything else like that. [*Husband*] I worked hard all my life. I don't ask any special favors. [*Wife*] I used to love a crowd around, but not anymore. It bothered Charles to have a crowd in the house. We used to take trips for the weekend; no more, nor summer picnics. It was physically impossible. We stopped.

[*Husband*] I worked that much harder. . . . I got mad on the job; used my hands on people; had to work it off with my body. I worked ten hours a day, seven days a week—construction work; got a reputation for roughness. . . . I was the kingpin, go where I wanted, work it off. I was wound up like a spring all the time. . . . [*Wife*] The reason we do not have any friends is me. I used to be good-natured, now I'm on the defensive. If anybody says anything against any group, I tell them off: "It is not democratic."

Even very outgoing couples curtailed their social life. One family traced the course of this change:

> [*Wife*] But actually we had a very normal household. We did a great deal of entertaining. At six o'clock he was put to bed and that was it. [*Husband*] I don't think it made any difference in our routine. . . . [*Wife*] When Richie was six years old, I had my mother upstairs needing complete 24-hour nursing care for three months. And it's still a home when guests come in. That was the only thing that was wrong—that we did run a big social life at the same time. [*Husband*] There was always a lot of activity. [*Wife*] We did continue to live what would be a perfectly normal life. (*turning to husband*) You could still call up from work and say you were going to bring company for lunch, and the meal would be ready.

But toward the end, as the problem grew grave, even this effiicient, energetic couple had to change their living patterns:

> [*Wife*] There was just one period when he came home from New Haven Hospital when he was six or seven until he went to Southbury at eight. He was so terrifically hyperactive. We had taken him as an emergency because Dr. Robinson had said, "Wrap him up in a blanket and rush him there." He had an acute heart condition; the doctor said heart failure brought on by the nephritis. When he was brought home, it was: "Keep him quiet for six months." [*Husband*] They advised bed care for six months. [*Wife*] Just like they do for rheumatic fever.
>
> They had him on phenobarbitol to keep him quiet and to prevent permanent heart damage, but he got a reverse reaction. He became so active; he got in this habit of running around. Only then we had only close friends in, not much else. Mostly it was myself; we had got out of the habit of much social. He was going to Southbury soon; I couldn't see breaking in a new babysitter. Then you don't have an eggnog party when he's hyperactive, running around the house wildly.

The parents of a dangerously hyperactive little girl sharply restricted their social activity; yet they tried to entertain anyway on the important occasions:

> We had a lot of New Year's Eve parties. She loved it. That was because everyone left her alone and she had free rein. Then with everyone feeling good they would go home and we would be up the rest of the night entertaining her.

Fatigue and strain from the arduous care of their hyperactive son curtailed the social activities of a strong gregarious couple:

[*Husband*] What the hell can you do? It was a madhouse here. We were so tired; we did not feel like seeing people, nobody! [*Wife*] At first, I did not feel like seeing nobody; I did not care whether anybody came or not. My good friends I told, "Come at night when he is asleep." I used to go to my club once a week, to church once a week in the evening.

Their older son, passing through the room, contributed, "Nobody had any extracurricular activities in this house until after 8 P.M., and then we were all too tired!"

Parenthetically, the husband recalled the infrequent help from others; they would "take him for a half hour and then 'Whoosh, can't stand this!' and one of the family would have to take over."*

Sometimes parents had to take turns going out; there might be no one to leave the retarded child with. One wife was matter-of-fact about it:

My husband would go if it was a wedding or something on his side of the family, and I would go if it was on my side.

But in another family the wife keenly regretted this:

What was bad for our personal relationships was that my husband had his activities; I had mine. . . . We had always done things together, lectures, concerts; and only now are we getting back to that companionship.

Still, it was probably better for parents to go out separately than to stay home together and mourn—or quarrel. And it was even more important to figure out ways for the mother to get away from the retarded child and the home, if only for brief periods. It was inevitable for mothers to have a preponderant burden of care of the retarded child. A father's usual response to this problem was to work harder, and thus spend more time away from home. It was not "natural" for most fathers to take over with the occasional care as they might have with a normal son or daughter.

And yet it was very important for a mother to get away. In a few families regular routines evolved to overcome the isolation of the mother. One solicitous husband made it possible for his wife to take a regular Saturday jaunt to the city—for shopping, a hairdo, and a show—while he took charge at home. Another perceptive husband even insisted that his wife work an evening shift at a nearby factory; he hurried home from work and took complete care of the child from suppertime to midnight.

* In Chapter 3 we described how the older brother and his pals took Frankie to the beach and how his father got up at 5 A.M. to care for him, how his older sister came home from college and took care of him and slept in the same room with him. Effective cooperation within this unusual core family brought the mother desperately needed relief.

Much of this evening time he spent riding around with his little girl in the automobile.

Taking a retarded child for leisurely auto rides over pleasant country roads or through the brightly lighted city was an activity that benefited almost every family. A mother explained:

> There were days when I just couldn't take it, say I would be away down in the dumps; he would take off from work, and we'd just ride.

She and her husband also discussed how they worked and planned together—including their retarded daughter in everything they did:

> [*Wife*] My husband took a swing shift so that he could be home to help do the shopping, groceries, bills, and so forth. My time was with the children. [*Husband*] For some four years we never went anywhere. [*Wife*] Having a child like that, no one is too pleased to stay with them. We didn't want to be obligated. If we went anywhere, we took her with us. We managed to take her to Maine one summer for two weeks. We thought the sun and air would be good for her. She loved the water.
>
> [*Husband*] She was a hard child to handle. [*Wife*] We understood how; and between my husband and I, we took her together. We always planned carefully and took her together. We never went where there were crowds. As to weddings, she wouldn't stay. It was by ourselves—a long ride, stop for ice cream, not to visiting or social occasions. Not any family visiting, if we could help it.
>
> Sometimes there would be a birthday party of a niece; if we didn't go, there would be hard feelings; they would think we were ashamed. We didn't want them to think that we didn't want to go because she was retarded, so we'd both take her, hold her close. You couldn't sit and talk; she was always jumping. We would leave early. She was happier here with her toys.

Another couple summed up their experience:

> [*Husband*] For years we couldn't visit people in their homes with our children . . . Freddy was destructive (not maliciously); and we were always afraid he would get into something or make a mess. People would urge us to come and bring him along, but we just didn't feel we could go through with it; it was asking too much. People never seemed to fully realize what a problem he was to take care of. [*Wife*] They would go by his normal appearance, how he looked sitting there in the car.

Many parents felt a need to include the retarded child in almost every family thing they did. Yet they would want to protect themselves and the retarded child from embarrassing encounters, so they would limit their social contacts to a few friends. They would choose occasions when the retarded child might be at his best, and go places where he had been happy before. They would not try new social activities with him without careful planning. To a point, this course of action was wise, sensibly protective. It conserved their energies and may have helped them keep their perspective.

Especially, parents learned to avoid social situations that brought a fresh reminder that their child was so sadly different. A father recalled glumly:

> Normal children would not play with him. We tried bringing him to the Christmas party at my club. He didn't stay. You feel bad, you see the rest doing all right. You get mad: "My kid can't enjoy it—to hell with it!"

Another father observed:

> The restriction is in places where the family goes out together among the public, such as a lodge or a church picnic. I never took my daughter. Half of my lodge brothers did not know that I had one.

This man, sociable by nature, found a satisfactory outlet for himself in fraternal and church activities but his wife withdrew:

> It did restrict my social life; I was inclined to want to stay home a lot more. (*turning to her husband*) More effect on me than on you!

Families who belonged to beach clubs or other associations for family recreation and sociability at a personal level found they could not comfortably include the retarded child even though he might have benefited from the activity. With the child in the picture, they just could not cope with the crowded intimacy that such an environment imposed. (Also, such close contact with a crowd would overstimulate the retarded child.)

However, when a retarded child was still young and tractable and when his parents' fortitude more than matched their sensitivity, they might take this child right out into the community. Quite a few fathers brought their retarded child out among an impersonal public. They patronized commercial recreation spots, public gathering places, concerts, and parades. They would feed pigeons on the Green, go to the playground or the beach at uncrowded hours, shop in market streets where the sales people were detached but kindly, even visit the firehouse or the detective bureau. The trainable child could enjoy these activities, and his father could, too, if he were not overly sensitive to an occasional curious stare.*

* This practice was most common in families with an only child or where the retarded child was much younger than his brothers or sisters. It would have less value if the parents made reluctant normal siblings join the party.

One older father with a mongoloid son described what they did:

> My recreation got to be taking him where he enjoyed going; parades especially he loved; and I did not mind the ball games. Before, I had gone down to the club a couple nights a week, but now I went down to the club with him just for a ride and to get him a soda, and take him home. . . . I took him all over. I had him out to the Yale Bowl half a dozen times. He loved it; he would yell and clap when the others did. He liked ball games, he liked music, he enjoyed the crowd. He was able to walk and to take care of himself. I even took him to the Yankee Stadium one Sunday. We sat way up at the top. He walked all the way up by himself. I took him to the Yale Bowl concerts. . . . I took him to all the parades—New Haven, East Haven, Branford; we went on the bus. . . . I'd ask him where he wanted to go. He'd prefer where he had been before. He'd ask, "When is the day for the parade?"

A courageous working-class couple, who together had devoted much time to training their active retarded boy, managed to include him in all their recreation and social activity: frequent outings to the movies, trips to the grandfather's home via intercity bus, pizza and hamburgers at a "high-class" restaurant where the proprietor let the little boy inspect the kitchen.

One young mother, a warm, outgoing person, took her retarded son and her younger child in a carriage regularly on long walks to the center of town, chatting with people along the way and explaining about the retardation:

> I would walk from here to East Haven and back with them. I met a lot of people through the children. Everyone who has met Todd along that way asks how Todd is coming along.

Many mothers took their young retarded children to the supermarket, wheeling them around in the basket cart while they shopped. The children loved it.

Gradually, though, as the retarded one grew older and bigger, more excitable and hence more erratic in his behavior, these parents stopped taking him out freely in the community. They would be troubled now by increasing unfriendly responses to his aberrant behavior. Even traits that they themselves had gotten used to, the little noises that went for speech, attracted unfavorable attention. Parents could tolerate an occasional awkward incident, but when embarrassment threatened on every occasion they stopped taking the child out among the public. And quite a few parents could never manage even impersonal relations in the community with their retarded child.

Whether the cause was the deviant behavior of the child, the lack of supportive friends and neighbors, or a sensitivity that wouldn't let the parents "make the public take him as he is," many parents did shy away from the community, or at least avoided any involvement there with their retarded child. They would only go out with him for a visit to the clinic, or a necessary fitting of new shoes, or a long overdue haircut (if a barber could be found who would do it).

Such parents were sometimes brought back into a partial relation with their community through joining the Association for Retarded Children. Hearing about support for legislation to help retarded children, sharing efforts to start little classes for the trainable, and meeting other people for whom getting a child's haircut was a major endeavor—all this served to lessen their isolation at a time when customary contacts were very difficult. For these families, getting involved *early* with the local ARC often brought tangible help and intangible comfort over the "rocky road" from discovery through commitment:

> [*Wife*] It got easier to talk after I joined the parents' association—when I understood how many people were in the same boat. . . . [*Husband*] Oh, yes, we talked about it before Wesley went to Southbury. We talk to anybody that seems interested. We raised money for the swimming pool. We wrote letters. We contacted a lot of people who did not know about Wesley's retardation.

A few of these parents continued their participation in the local Association for Retarded Children long after their own child's commitment. Perhaps this just fulfilled a desire on their part to be of service in this cause. Perhaps it reflected a continuing need for informal sociability with other families who understood what it meant to live with this problem. Sometimes there resulted lasting friendships. One father went so far as to say:

> Today our companionship is limited to other parents of retarded children. They are intellectually and socially above the average.

On the other hand, some parents were reluctant to participate in an organization devoted to a problem so emotion-laden for them. Some found more effective outlets elsewhere for the personal needs ARC seeks to serve. But at some stage almost everyone got some help from a parents' group contact.

Most of these families were church members. Where they held strong religious convictions, they continued to do so, but their participation might diminish, especially as a family group. Said a mother:

> To tell you the truth, I never went when I had Joey. Father came to find out why. He said, "You have a problem; you take care of him; if his father can stay with him once in a while, you come then if you can." He understood. I go now, though.

A few of these retarded children themselves had an opportunity to participate in church worship and activities, abetted by pastoral kindliness and consideration. One little mongoloid boy who had the freedom of the neighborhood felt welcome in the parish church. He went every day, often by himself, attending with equal piety weddings, Masses, funerals.

Positive religious faith was a source of strength. One family put it this way:

> [*Wife*] We always got there. That was our morale. [*Husband*] We never missed Mass unless we were so sick we couldn't move. [*Wife*] You have to have something to keep you together. I don't see how anyone could last if they didn't have the church.

Another husband expressed it:

> It was probably the most important stabilizing factor, our religion. We were mad at one another with this thing, whether we realized it or not.

A mother observed:

> We didn't blame God for it. Every night I say a prayer for them at the training school that they will have the patience and understanding to take care of her and of those other kids up there.

A very few did blame God for it; one mother told how she moved from religious alienation to excess:

> I hated God. I did not want to hear anything. Then I went from one extreme to the other. Two years ago I joined a religious organization—Jehovah's Witnesses. They study the Bible. I've been reading the Bible all the way through. I argued with them, though. I don't agree with all their beliefs. I'd read the Bible to my husband when he was shaving! Now I'm back to normal. It got me thinking about religion again, anyway. We went every Sunday before we had the kids. We were Episcopalian.

Even parents with staunch convictions who regularly attended church could be highly critical of the behavior of certain clerics or troubled at the indifference of their church institutions. One family recalled:

> [*Husband*] I was worried. I was afraid I might lose my wife. From our own religion we got no help or counsel. [*Wife*] The priest would not even make a call for me. We got no sympathy and no help from our own. [*Husband*] We got very little help from the church. . . . They'd say, "Go to the state institutions"—when there was no place for her. . . . You handle it through your own church agencies and you get no sympathy and no help!

Another father volunteered:

As far as the Italian-born priests were concerned, this was a thing for us to accept and say nothing of it. The American priests would talk with you about it, have some sympathy. Not the ones who were born in Italy—they knew nothing of it. They said we should feel honored because God gave us an angel.

Another father, similarly admonished by his priest, commented:

I told him I'd rather have her home committing a few sins than up there where she is.

A Protestant couple remembered:

[*Wife*] It restricted us a good many years from going to church. We had had her at Sunday School when she was little. The minister we had then did not seem to care about problems like that. . . . [*Husband*] That minister was there to minister to the spiritual needs of the normal. Now Dr. Kipp was different. I think the ministry *can* be a great help. "I never realized you had a problem like that," he said. He arranged for a place for Brian [the normal brother] to live out in Arizona. We sent him out there on a plane when he was seventeen.

Church or sect, Catholic or Protestant, there was no positive policy then toward retardation, so it was the response of the individual priest or minister that counted with these families.

This problem affected the family stance toward the world outside. Out in the community these families behaved differently from normal families. Significantly, at a time in their lives when young parents ordinarily attain maximum involvement in activities outside the home, the pressures of this problem limited the social commitments and participation of every one of these families. Some families completely withdrew; other limited their outside involvement to the necessary instrumental contacts that their situation demanded, or to social activity that was comfortable and feasible. Their ties became tenuous. They did not make much of a contribution to community life, nor did they draw on community resources even for such reduced benefits as were available to their family.

Chapter 6

Waiting for a Place at Southbury

The commitment of a retarded child to the care of the state was a very hard thing to do. Parents did think of it as "putting their child away." Almost all of these families took more than a year, some much longer, before they reached the decision to apply for the training school. They had been told that there was a long waiting list, there would be a delay. Yet they did not apply earlier because they just were not ready.

Sometimes family circumstances justified keeping a tractable child at home longer, beyond pre-school age. An older mother in a large, old-fashioned close-knit family, after eighteen years of marriage had finally given birth to a son who proved to be a mongoloid of relatively high level. They had no family doctor or regular pediatrician. Admonitions from the clinic doctors they occasionally went to always conveyed a recommendation for commitment, but without any reference to the positive things Southbury could offer such a child. The mother reacted:

> You wouldn't mind if you had another child. Your mind is always on him. I did take him to St. Raphael's to the children's clinic at six. They told me to have him go to Southbury. . . . Every doctor we ever had him to said, "Southbury is the only place for him. That child should never stay home; you should send him to the training school." . . . But I had to take care of him; he was my son. . . . We tried everything to teach him. My sister tried to teach him; she would put the pencil in his hand; she would try very hard. I didn't know much of the place Southbury. I thought it was terrible to part with him at six.

There were some parents who made a first tentative step under their doctor's urging and reassurance: "Put her application in. When the time comes for her to be admitted you can refuse if you want to." Some cautious ones made an early application, planning to follow through *only* if their family situation changed radically. Generally, though, only after the shock of discovery had blunted with time and the family problem of the retarded child become aggravated did most families move at all to press an application for commitment. There was no typical sequence, but the following account is representative:

[*Husband*] You mean [how we reacted] when Dr. Samsel said she should be put away—well, when he first told us, we were against it. I made her room all white tileboard, screening over the windows, so we thought we could keep her. [*Wife*] I didn't approve of putting her away. Definitely, that was out! It was my problem, and I was going to do it. That was my life; that was it! [*Husband*] Matter of fact, we didn't think of putting her away until she got so big and strong we couldn't tackle it. . . . I think it took longer to convince my wife than it did me. She didn't get any worse; she just got bigger and stronger. . . . We couldn't manage her any more. [*Wife*] She was too big; she could knock me over.

He was a vigorous man, and his wife a strong, efficient woman. This vital, intelligent couple had postponed too long—beyond the time when any family could control a child such as theirs, temperamental and possessed of a violent energy. (Sometimes, the stronger the parents, the longer they persisted in struggling with a severely retarded child at home.)

This family should have had much earlier the help of a counselor whom they could trust. Through the years when the retarded child remains at home, the continuing role of the counselor is critically important —not so much in directly persuading the parents to move toward a placement decision, but in helping them to see clearly the realities of their child's present and future status and to realize that "he can be helped only as Southbury can do it." Some counselors did succeed in presenting the Southbury placement as an opportunity for training to which the child was entitled, a group living experience where he would find companionship.

When families enjoyed a constant relationship with the same doctor over these years, they were better able to carry their burden until the problem was resolved somehow. They came to trust their doctor's judgment: "I probably wouldn't have placed him so early if it wasn't for Dr. Naylor. My conscience was clear." Several busy general practitioners and pediatricians took pains to work with families in an individual fashion.

It helped, too, when the doctor had acquired a clear knowledge of the total family situation. Sometimes the doctor as counselor had to be rather blunt to be effective. One husband's reluctance to sign the application was finally overcome by straight talk from their old family physician:

Your wife is going to go crazy, and you'll have her in one place and your kid in another. If you leave the kid home, your wife is going to have to go away.

Now, families could no longer have valid reservations concerning an authoritative prognosis. They could not be allowed to emotionally reject the implications of a bleak outlook. And yet the very hopelessness of some of these cases caused parents to keep on searching, to want to try anything:

> We even took her to a brain doctor, to operate—even if she didn't survive! He said there was nothing to operate on. We took her to eighteen doctors.

Some doctors at the clinics were abrupt, impatient at the parents' inability to take their quick counsel, to see what was quite obvious. They did use harsh terms to shock the parents into realization. One mother recalled her unhappy contacts with clinic doctors, which she continued long after she had been told of the retardation and advised to place her child:

> A social worker from Hartford was going to take her to the St. Raphael Clinic [at nine years old]. From waiting in the cold room on the table, Estelle was cold and upset before the doctor arrived.
>
> "Your daughter is like a beautiful Cadillac, but no motor and four flat tires," Dr. Colby said. I wanted to tell him about her, with me holding her she could go up and down stairs, play patty-cake too.
>
> You have to take a lot of insults, even from a doctor. Dr. Kaplan told me when she was three years old, "Your daughter is like a vegetable." He made me go out of there crying. . . .
>
> Another incident—we took Estelle to Newington, the first child to be looked at. Again Dr. Colby: "There is no use of me examining this child. I examined her before." This sort of gave me a jolt. "Are you Christ on the Cross? Don't you think my child could have changed since the last time?" I said. My husband was there, took the day off. Frances the baby was there. I was pregnant with another child, which I lost. You have to take such insults.

In recounting these incidents, this mother became much distressed; she was apologetic recalling her language to the doctor. In retrospect, she was rueful about her pertinacity:

> To be truthful, I did not want to know the truth. I felt it was an insult if anybody told me that my child was retarded. I had not known enough about it to realize that Estelle was connected with them.

Succinctly, another mother recalled her experience:

> At a little over three, I took him to the Cerebral Palsy Clinic; Dr. Tucker was very abrupt, and he didn't know how to tell the parents. The mothers would come out in tears. He made me too mad to cry. I felt like turning around and fighting for the child.

Whatever their social status, parents all reacted in the same way to a brusque impersonal encounter at the clinic. A middle-class father was distressed:

> You go into the clinic; first there is a misconception that they can do something about it—not just a testing. You were only going for advice. It is just a testing laboratory; they do not give you advice. Then the tests are so fast and mechanical. It's a shock, the speed of it—and not much confidence in the "young squirts" making the tests, young laboratory technicians who seemed not overly competent. Then they come, shrug their shoulders, "No help for you."
>
> You go out of there thinking that the world has collapsed around you, and that it has been done by inferior people. . . . There is still resentment in our minds that they are fast, crude, and unkind. . . . Whereas, if they had said, "We will need time to evaluate, consultations," and then had had someone talk to us the next day who looked responsible, it would have been better.

However, some doctors at the clinics succeeded in inspiring trust in the parents. A father, who could say nothing good about anyone else, warmly respected the staff at the Yale Medical School Child Development Clinic:

> We went back twice a month to the Clinic. . . . You couldn't go much better.

A mother conveyed her growing confidence in the psychiatrist at the Yale Child Study Center:

> The only thing that reassured me was that Dr. Guertin had told me that any kind person could take our place. Marcia didn't regard us in the same way as normal children do their parents. . . . After I had digested that fact, I was more resigned. . . . From what Dr. Guertin said, it would be a lifetime proposition. . . . The consolation now is that she will be cared for whether we are there or not.

Social workers, also, played an important part in helping the parents toward commitment. Sometimes a tactful social worker, sympathetic but clear-headed, could help reluctant parents to organize their knowledge and feelings about their retarded child and work their way through to their own decision. A hard-pressed mother commented:

> The Visiting Nurse and the Family Service helped me quite a bit to make the decision, but mostly the Family Service. . . . They did write quite a few letters . . . [about getting Geoffrey into Southbury], and they could get satisfaction.

As the waiting period lengthened, social workers continued helpful: advising, comforting, making contacts for the parents.

People other than professionals often helped in this decision process. By the time the need for institutional care became pressing, close friends and relatives who had helped sustain the family would aid in clarifying their decision for placement.

A young mother said:

Before, I didn't want to even hear of Southbury or speak of it. I wanted to keep her home, not put her anywhere. Our friends told us, "At this time she is like a baby, but as she gets older, she would have habits, do more mischief." . . . My father said, "It must be a good place Southbury, but you must make up your own mind, decide for yourself. If you're going to send her up there and cry every day over it, you'd better really decide for yourself."

Another family sought guidance from several sources; the mother described it:

I asked my friends about Southbury when first Dr. Farnham had told me Frankie would never be a normal child. One of my friends took me up there to see her boy. His cottage was in the Village. I cried, but she said, "See how nice it is! You will feel better about it by and by." . . . Dr. Samsel and Dr. Farnham had said, "Frankie will get along fine at Southbury. He will like it there." My aunt, a nurse, had said, "Mary, do not be foolish; put him in. Someday he will be so rough that from love you'll grow to hate him. Do not wait until it's too late." . . . Everybody was for it: "If anything should happen to you he would have to go." "He better go when I am healthy and can still love him, not later when I could not stand him." "Send him now when he is young and will get used to it."

One mother, recounting the minor crisis that led to commitment of her profoundly retarded infirm infant, revealed the major role the grandmother had played in this decision:

On the day of my birthday we had gone out for dinner, and my mother had a very hard time with the baby and with herself. She thought if anything happened to her, who would help with the baby?

The grandmother finished the story:

I came back from a funeral. Phil was upstairs with a boy friend taking care of the baby. Before I could get into the house, he called out to me, "Nana, I'm going. I have to go out." I thought to myself that it wasn't his responsibility really. Children don't want responsibility. Why let it go further? I went down and used the phone and called David Kline and Mr. Olesky.

The next day I asked them both if they were willing still to let the baby go. I said, "You've got to give me an answer one way or another. You contact Mr. Olesky."

Usually, one spouse was ahead of the other about commitment. Many times it was the husband who lagged, but sometimes a husband would say, "I was the biggest persuader where my wife was concerned. She couldn't see it."

A couple discussed this more fully:

[*Husband*] Had it been my decision, Freddy would have been at Southbury much earlier; but I decided to let it ride until my wife was ready. First I tried to push her, but then I decided to just wait. [*Wife*] I just did not feel he should go at all. . . . I had not accepted it really yet; I thought he was going to be better than predicted. I was waiting until seven years; they always had those articles that stressed the big change at age seven.

[*Husband*] I guess I gave up hoping for improvement long before you did. When he was seven and a half, I filed an application. I didn't waste any time. [*Wife*] When I became willing. . . . I just found it within myself finally. My girl friend, the nurse, helped. She said there are a lot of cases that are not up in the front in any institution; and they get just as good care. It was just the accumulation of things; it was affecting everything too much. I think everybody gets to the point where they can no longer take it. I told my husband I thought it was going to be him or me going away.

Another mother resisted long and stubbornly, despite the pressure of friends and relatives:

[*Wife*] Yes, we've heard that: "If it was my kid, I'd put her away." . . . They would holler at me for devoting my life to her, day and night, without a break. Mostly sympathetic criticism, but I resented it. It was my child and I was doing it. If they did not like it, they didn't need to come again. I got so I hated to hear the doorbell ring—someone else coming complaining! . . .

[*Husband*] They were trying to educate us that it would be better for *us*. They had not had experience with Southbury; but they had seen what this had done to other families who tried to keep them home. Since my daughter has been away I go out of my way to talk to anyone who has a child like that, to tell them about Southbury, to try to persuade them. I personally think we made a mistake that we didn't let her go the first time.

Sometimes people quite remote in their relationship played a strategic part in guiding the family to the Southbury decision. One couple in replying to the question: "Who is the person who helped you most to make the decision to send your child to Southbury?" gave the following account:

[*Wife*] Nate Etzel—the Jewish fellow—brought us up to Southbury Training School to see it. [*Husband*] A salesman who came to my father's store helped me to contact him. [*Wife*] Then there was Marie. At this outing at Rockwell Park we went to, Carlotta was dashing around to different tables. This one woman was very nice to Carlotta, because she already had a daughter at Southbury. She sat Carlotta down at their table and started giving her an I.Q. test, like they had given her child at Southbury. Then she said to me: "Did you ever think of sending your child to Southbury? She will do very well there; there is a lot of difference between her and

> my child." [Did you mind her suggestion?] [*Husband*] She was in our condition so we appreciated it. [*Wife*] She and her husband helped us a lot. [*Husband*] Her and Mr. Etzel helped us the most to make up our minds to send Carlotta to Southbury. She said, "You'll be very foolish if you don't send her. You'll be sorry later." She helped us to go through the ropes.

Apart from the influence of other people, there were internal factors that made parents push the application. The resources of the family might have been dissipated. The health of the mother or father might have deteriorated. Said one mother:

> I had gotten so rundown that I had to have X-rays every month; they feared T.B. There were three children at home, including a baby.

Another mother, though she insisted that her retarded son had been no trouble, came to the decision because of her own waning strength and the heavy demands of her role as wife and mother:

> I didn't even want to put him on the list at first, but after the third baby was born, I sincerely knew I couldn't do it. It might have been when he was three years old, but I think it was later. I was worn thin, on the verge of a nervous breakdown. The two youngest were 15 months apart. Then I threw in the towel. I'd be cross with the middle one in trying to protect Daniel, the oldest. It didn't seem to be fair. I couldn't do it alone—if I had had some help! But I was losing my patience with all of them. Poor Benjamin was getting caught in the middle.

One mother's attitude against commitment gradually softened under the impact of her son's dangerous hyperactivity:

> At age three I didn't accept quite yet that he could be that bad. . . . At five years old he was unmanageable. I couldn't take care of him safely any more. You couldn't trust him anywhere—lights, stove, cars. I did not make the application until I knew I couldn't take care of him any more at home.

Often the care of the retarded child abruptly became too much for his family. Sometimes it was the increasing hyperactivity of the child; sometimes it was the aggravated infirmity or illness. A child's seizures might have become more frequent and more severe. The total condition of the child might have gravely deteriorated.

In some cases the parents only followed through because they feared the death of the child. One such family had postponed sending their infirm son to Southbury because, as the father said:

> It is like setting out a poor little helpless rabbit. So many kids! Beds, beds, beds! I thought, "Somebody will poke him. . . . What

> could they do for him up there? It would be getting rid of him. He could not compete with anyone." We seriously considered it only when Charles began to fail [at age fourteen]. . . .
>
> If he did not get the medical care, he would die. I sat there with him one night when I had gotten up with him. He used to sit in the chair all day, and when he lay down at night the muscles in his legs would cramp and he'd cry. I had gotten up with him that night. I sat there with him all night and convinced myself I had to take him to Southbury. I said to him, "I'll *have* to send you to school, Buster."

When the focus of the afflicted child's problem was medical, seriously so, the parents did accept the fact that Southbury could do what they could no longer do for this beloved child at home—provide the continuous care and the hospital environment that he needed. They knew now that they could not achieve their goal of keeping him always with the family.

And when their child's behavior had become uncontrollable, dangerously hyperactive, parents did accept that he needed the institution for the custodial control and protective training which a family cannot provide at home. One father expressed it:

> We just realized that it was a matter of care for the rest of his life. We hoped that they might teach him to be useful and take on some little duties.

Parents now came to realize that an early estimate of "50 percent retarded" [sic] did not mean that their daughter would function as a normal seven-year-old when she attained the chronological age of fourteen. They understood now the frightening significance of the gap between their child's physical maturity and his infinitely lower mental and emotional development. They had acquired a more accurate view of his probable future status. But it was still difficult for them to put much of this realization into words; some parents, hedging a little, could still say, "Science may find something; there's always the possibility of a miracle," although they really did not believe this.

From the beginning—at discovery or earlier—there had been a repeated giving up of hopes and goals for their child, and perhaps for themselves. As the time of commitment to Southbury neared, the expectations most parents really did have for their child were modest: They hoped that he would somehow make an adjustment to Southbury Training School, that he would be kindly treated and find security and comfort there.

They hoped that he would have an opportunity to attend school, a class for the trainable. They hoped that he could be trained in simple work skills, "that he might learn to work with his hands, or anything so that he could sit down and do something."

They hoped that their severely retarded child would learn some self-care, profit from the habit-training he might receive. They hoped very much that through being with his own kind he might be less isolated, even enjoy some sociability with his peers. They hoped that the cottage personnel would understand his wants and needs if he couldn't tell them.

An especial hope for a hyperactive child was:

> If he'd just get to quiet down and learn to take care of himself so that he would be able to go out and walk among the trees! Then I'd be satisfied.

The most sanguine, yet not entirely unfounded hope expressed by parents was that their child might some time later, having profited from the Southbury training, return home when his brothers and sisters had grown up and gone out on their own.

After families had gotten over the hurdle of applying, they had to wait for a place. The waiting period was apt to be very long—a year at least, sometimes two or more. During this time the facilities of the state training schools in Connecticut were strained to accommodate an expanding population. It was more than a matter of bed space; the ratio of patients to staff had increased so sharply as to interfere with the effective organization of the school. Accordingly, admissions were restricted to emergency cases. Families were loath to press for admission until indeed theirs became an emergency, either through their child's deteriorated condition or their own suffering and depleted resources.

This waiting was an added strain factor affecting family behavior. Some parents were tempted to withdraw their application as months passed and future uncertainty preyed on them. Their feelings about sending their child away were mixed. Said one mother:

> I think it was harder once the decision had been made. I was anxious for it to come to pass, but when there was the indecision as to when—then I didn't want him to go. Half of me wanted the day to come and get it over with, the other half didn't. I got so exhausted.

Inevitably, parents and siblings too had ambivalent feelings toward the retarded child. The time of waiting for commitment accentuated this ambivalence. A mother would feel that she could not hold out another week, and then would doubt again whether she was doing the right thing in placing her child with the state. Although the retarded child's condition and behavior tended to worsen over this period, yet there were times when things seemed to go passably well at home, when the child was tractable, happy, perhaps mastering some important little tasks that before had eluded him. Then it was possible for parents to feel the fleeting question: "Is he improving? Is he learning? May he not become easier to care for?" If this were a child who strongly related to his family (many parents were sure that their trainable children did), then it was hard to reconcile a deep longing to cherish this winsome, fun-loving, needing child at home with an objective view of him as an incompetent, arrested personality whose actions jeopardized the survival of the family—and who must be sent away.

Ambivalence varied widely among families. Perhaps it was most disruptive for those aggressive parents who themselves had suffered harsh, insecure lives. In any event, our data do suggest that the factors underlying ambivalence are to be found in the family background and in the personalities of the individual members. Some parents saw their child almost simultaneously from a highly subjective viewpoint of desperate protective affection and also through eyes not quite objective but reflecting the way that others must have viewed him.

There were aggravated problems associated with the retarded child's continued presence in the home. The health of the mother might be impaired during these years of waiting, and there were usually other young children in the home with demands to be met. A mother was pregnant with her seventh child:

> [*Wife*] Help was scarce—a visiting nurse or a little domestic help. I have no family to call on. My mother is in New York City. My husband would take his vacation when I had the babies so that he would be home to help. You couldn't put Marcia to bed. When Jean Ann, the youngest, was coming along, I had no place to keep her from Marcia; Marcia got so she could climb the baby gate. I was afraid I would lose the new baby. I needed proper rest. I had the phlebitis which I had gotten because I kept on nursing Shirley, the eldest girl, when I shouldn't have. . . . (The nurse had neglected to relay the doctor's orders.) I wear elastic stockings because of it. The doctor kept telling me "rest and proper diet." I lost all my top teeth. We were really desperate, back against the wall. . . .
>
> [*Husband*] From then on, more fits, lost more sleep, the tension was building up. [*Wife*] I was just hoping my strength would hold out. I was just so far gone. I hoped she would be admitted before anything happened to her or the new baby. Jean Ann was just starting to walk. [*Husband*] Time was running out.

A physically growing child whose behavior stayed about the same would cause distress and annoyance to his family and the neighbors. Eccentric actions that in a three-year-old elicited good-humored tolerance would receive a harsher response when done by an eight-year-old. Although a retarded child might not change much, his family did. The total family situation never improved. If the parents were older, their vigor and resilience were ebbing. One mother conveyed this:

> Before he went away I used to live in fear. I'd get up every morning and wonder, "What will happen today?" . . . I do not want ever again to experience that feeling. In this time he seemed to be even more mischievous. . . . I just could not take it anymore; nor my husband. I knew I wasn't helping him any more. I almost threw the social worker out of the house, I was so upset. She told me to wait, to be patient. I couldn't wait any longer for some help. She said, "Don't get upset." I told her, "I get so sick of you people; you just come and talk." . . . When I felt I could not keep him another week, this social worker recommended that I look at Racebrook, near my old home. I wouldn't put him there. They had no help, one nurse and a colored boy for so many. Filthy cots—$125 a month. I came home crying when I saw those other little children all grouped up and just one woman taking care of them. We waited another year, and glad to get Southbury.

In most of these cases the behavior of the severely retarded child did not remain constant over the months and years of waiting for a place at Southbury. As the more capable of these children reached school age they experienced increasing difficulty coping with their environment at home. One family described their son's reaction:

> [*Wife*] Those years were terrible and very trying years. It was terrific to handle Richie. That panic of his running into the woods! There was an element of embarrassment in the police being called out to look for him. . . . If it hadn't been for the neighbors, he would have wandered off more. The neighbor children didn't present a problem; Richie presented the problem. He couldn't keep up with them and so he would wander off. Quite often you'd see him out playing with the kids, and then he'd be off by himself the next time you looked.
>
> [*Husband*] And Andy the younger brother was coming along getting ready to go to school. Richie knew he was older and yet he couldn't go. When Andy started to go to school, it was more of a problem. . . . I don't think Richie was as happy at home in that period. He has peculiar insight on what's going on. He would hang out by the orchard; my wife would call him and offer him an apple or some ice cream. He would cover his ears and wouldn't answer her, make believe he wasn't home. Then when Andy would come home from kindergarten, Richie would rush in too and say, "Where's the ice cream, Mommy?" as though he had been away at school too—at his school in the orchard.

In another family there was a daughter:

> [*Wife*] She was very hard to take care of. She would run off and disappear, even if she had other children to play with. . . . In 1945 —we had applied for Southbury and before Mike was born—she

disappeared when we lived in Hamden. She was lost and the cops picked her up in North Haven near the railroad tracks. They couldn't find out where she lived. [*Husband*] I thought perhaps a 100 percent disabled "psycho," an ex-Marine, had taken her. . . . They mature earlier; she'd disappear; all you could wonder was what would happen when she got older. I knew eventually it would have to come to that [commitment]. If you rationalize it out, it is the only way.

A large working-class family had kept their retarded eldest son at home until age sixteen, abandoning an earlier application. Quite trainable, and of a quiet friendly nature, this boy had responded to his parents' solicitous care and discipline. They reapplied when in his midteens he started to wander:

> [*Wife*] I had already had his name in for Southbury before anything happened. I wanted him to have some training. Right after I got his name on, I thought he would go. Then he started getting in trouble taking wagons. He would take and stay out late, refuse to come in. [*Husband*] He would be over in Edgewood Avenue Park; he would be all over. If he saw you coming for him, he would run and try to hide on you. We would send the kids looking for him; then we would go ourselves.
>
> We had got him sold on the idea of going away to school; and he kept on waiting and waiting, and it did not come through; so he got kind of disgusted. I used to tell him, "Stay in the house tomorrow night," as a punishment if he had gone off and stayed late. He minded pretty good, but all of a sudden he would go again.

These moderately retarded children became frustrated at their inability to enter into the life around them and to interact effectively with other children. It was as if they, too, were conscious of the widening gap between their normal counterparts and themselves. They *knew* their behavior did not meet the expectations of the important other people in their lives. Runnnng away, unpredictable tantrums, and periodic hyperactive behavior arose out of such frustrations. Sometimes when emotionally upset, they became destructive.

Infirm and profoundly retarded children became a greater physical and social burden to their families as they approached adolescence. Children whose severe mental defect was associated with other organic impairment declined in health and vitality during these years. If they were subject to seizures, the incidence of these became more frequent and severe. One mother described this:

> I was close to sheer exhaustion. The convulsions were getting worse; and Martha would go from one to another. I couldn't pull her out of them. She was staying close to a coma. A couple times we had to take her to the emergency room of the hospital.

Severe forms of cerebral palsy, mongolism complicated by heart disorder, progressive neural degeneration—these and kindred pathologies brought about a situation in the home where even young and capable parents were hard pressed to manage (and these were the very ones who had to wait the longest to place their child).

Meanwhile, to maintain some sort of equilibrium in the home, the families made further changes in their living patterns. Some were changes dictated by the increasing demands the retarded child made on his family. Others were adaptations that anticipated the child's removal from the home. At this time there might be an effort to prepare the mother for the separation and conserve her waning strength. There was often a rearrangement of the division of labor in the home. Some fathers took on more family chores or devoted more of their away-from-work time to the retarded child, freeing the mother for other family roles, or even outside activities. One mother went to work in a factory, a second shift that would dovetail with her husband's work schedule. She told about the arrangements:

> Then my kid sister would come in and take care of her for two hours between the time when I went to work and when my husband came home. This was for a period of over a year, up until Southbury. My sister did a wonderful job with her. She was only thirteen years old.

Her husband added:

> She would change her. Nights when I'd take Margaret to ride she would come along to help.

Sisters, young cousins, or other relatives were now employed regularly to sit for a few hours. A few couples had young married friends, as yet childless, who would stay with the retarded child occasionally to provide the parents an opportunity to go out together. Parents lacking family help at this stage might call upon a neighbor to stand by, when there was no actual care involved, to "listen" when the child was asleep upstairs, "to be there in case of fire." Now that everyone knew about their child's retardation and their plans for Southbury, it was easier to accept this help.

Only two of the retarded children in this study could participate in the little activity programs which voluntary associations were just then starting for trainable children. However, some parents were able to engage the services of young pre-professionals for relief child care. Student teachers or nurses were quite willing to do this part-time work. The esprit of the eager beginner and the practical value of the experience would offset any reluctance to care for an abnormal child.

With the separation of the retarded child imminent, parents might suddenly realize that they had been short-shrifting their other children and neglecting one another. There was apt to be renewed concern now for the needs of all the family members, especially when husband and wife were in agreement on the Southbury placement. Whenever they could somehow find the time and the energy, families turned their attention to meeting these other needs. One family obtained early psychiatric help for a bright little girl much upset about her retarded brother. By the time of his placement she had benefitted and was doing well in school. A mother made contingent plans to put her expected new baby in a foundling home until the commitment of her retarded child. Some parents tried to make positive long-range plans for the future. One family completed arrangements to care for foster children in their home as soon as their own child should be placed, and explored the possibilities of adoption. Several other families subsequently did take foster children, in part to provide companionship for the siblings left at home.

In several cases during the time of waiting, family survival made necessary an abrupt, temporary placement of a severely retarded and ill child in whatever private facility was available.* This was more apt to happen with a family who had long delayed in applying or lost their place on the list by refusing a placement opportunity. The arrival of a new baby or the illness of one of the parents were precipitating causes.

This was a very drastic measure. The relief it brought scarcely outweighed the heavy emotional and financial burden such a makeshift arrangement imposed on a family. And such a temporary placement in a private-for-profit hospital might turn out to be of dangerously long duration, threatening to become permanent:

> Two days before Jim was born, she went to Marlowe. My husband and I were terribly upset all the time she was there. . . .The year at Marlowe was a mess; if she had stayed there much longer she wouldn't have lasted. I did not realize until recently when she is well and happy at Southbury what a great difference it had made in our lives. . . . The Marlowe year was the worst, and he was working nights and Saturdays to pay for it. . . .
>
> I had wondered: "Should I have the baby at home, or should I take Martha to the hospital with me?" I hadn't had a full night's sleep for about a year before that. She was so much care; we couldn't easily find a place for Martha. . . . If I had it to do over again she'd never go to Marlowe—not for what it did to our lives, but for the lack of care she suffered. I dreaded having my husband go up there

* As will be seen, this was quite different from an early plan to send the child to a special school, or from placing a severely retarded newborn in a nursery boarding home. None of our families took this last way, but two had been advised to and almost did place mongoloid babies at birth.

> when she was at Marlowe. She was losing weight, and looked so neglected. After visiting her on a Sunday I'd come out and sit in the car and cry for fifteen minutes before I could drive home. My husband hadn't accepted yet the fact of her being away. If I should bring her back home, he wouldn't let her go to Southbury. Up at Marlowe kids were lying in wet puddles on a rubber drawsheet; they were tied to their cribs. Finally my mother-in-law insisted on going with me. We consoled each other and came home and lied to my husband. . . .
>
> You walked in that back part and it was terrible. The whole place was. You walked in that back part; they had her in a storeroom. . . . My mother-in-law and I used to give the attendants a dollar or so to take better care of Martha. They were understaffed; the turnover was terrific. Martha had a diaper rash from the middle of her back to the middle of her stomach for six weeks. Just a rubber drawsheet to lie on.

This was a desperate case, and yet the family had to wait a full year for Southbury. The admissions office of the training school justifiably gave priority to hardship cases where a family was still struggling to cope with their child at home. After all, any kind of a placement away was a solution of sorts; a home by this time might provide no solution at all.

There were other reasons why for some families the waiting period lengthened. Reference has been made to parents who had first applied without any firm intent. For these families the waiting period was apt to be very long, particularly if at some time they had rejected the proffer of an immediate placement. If their rejection of this offer had been hostile, future relations between parents and the admissions office might be strained.

Very sad were those cases in which the parents did firmly intend commitment at the earliest possible time, but meanwhile courageously and quite effectively adapted and carried on with the retarded child at home. Their record of successful coping might result in unwarranted delay in admitting the retarded child later on when the family's resources for providing care had been exhausted. Unless such courageous parents had kept up a steady pressure on the admissions office, they were apt to be passed over in favor of a family whose "hollering" had been more effective than their coping. The absence of other young children in the home was also a factor that led to the prolonging of the waiting period, probably by both parties, state and family.

Parents rarely complained, though, of inequity in the admissions process. It appeared that the director and the social workers charged with this responsibility of deciding among families acted fairly. This admissions office, understaffed though it was, also provided occasional effective support and counsel to the families on the emergency waiting list.

There were some factors that probably accelerated the commitment. The actual suffering of the family was the principal one. The ability of a family, including the severely retarded child himself, to graphically portray their predicament was another. In one instance, a retarded child put on a terrific exhibition of hyperactivity that convinced the visiting social worker on the spot.

A third factor was a capacity to maintain continuing effective communication between family and state agency. A father recalled:

> It was one and a half years we were waiting for the new cottage. They had put him on the emergency list, and then when they reviewed it, they put Freddy on their quicker list. I acted on the theory of the wheel that squeaks the loudest; I would call Mrs. Simpson or Miss Nuzzo, the social worker, every three or four months. If the social worker didn't get around right on time every six months I would call and say, "We need some help and advice down here." I was afraid he would get severely hurt before he did go.

Said a mother:

> Finally, my daughter wrote a lovely letter explaining just what Frankie did from 5 A.M. to night. We got a nice letter back, and in a month he was in.

In summary, this waiting period was difficult for all, and terribly hard for those families who had deferred too long a decision to place their child. There probably had been sharper suffering in the weeks immediately following discovery, but this year or more of waiting was filled with a deep despair and sense of failure.* Fewer than a third of these families had any helpful orientation to the training school during this time; and not even all of these could be reassured. Most parents just felt they were sacrificing the retarded child to save the rest of the family. They could not conceive that any positive good could result for their afflicted child. This was their view, however well or ill the actual commitment process went.

* Yet, it must be said that the absence of any waiting period might be undesirable. Evidently, whatever their expressed feelings and reactions, families continued to work through in their lives this radical decision to commit their child while they were waiting—now pressing for an early admission and now wondering if in placement they were doing the right thing.

Chapter 7

And Finally, Commitment of the Severely Retarded Child

> Toward the end I started feeling sorry for myself, "I'm getting older and I'm tired." I'd be over it in five or ten minutes. I figured it was my duty. It was very sad. It was harder. You'd think there was a funeral. There was nothing in my house, no music, no nothing. I loved Estelle more that last couple months than I did all the time I had her. I figured they wouldn't understand her little sounds and signs. I knew when she wanted to drink, to move her bowels, wanted a toy. I thought they wouldn't have that patience. I was trying to make her walk, so she wouldn't have to go; I was trying to smarten her up, get words to come out of her mouth. . . .
>
> I had the papers home for over a month. I didn't know what I was supposed to do with them, but I didn't try to find out. I guess I did it on purpose. I found all sorts of reasons—I couldn't find the papers. They called from Southbury to see if we wanted her to go.

The letter that finally came from Hartford from the head of the admissions office was matter-of-fact, announcing there was a bed now ready for the retarded child, mentioning in some detail the clothing the family should provide and then outlining the legal procedures involved—and how the family must handle the papers. There had to be a hearing before the judge of the Probate Court. The forms had to be sent up to Hartford to await the governor's signature. Then a day could be set for bringing the child to Southbury. If the social worker during a recent visit had been able to prepare the family for these steps it did help.

The process of commitment was unwieldy, confusing, and subject to delay. It was impersonal, too, and that added to their fears that their child wouldn't be treated as an individual. One mother was concerned:

> . . . that they would rub his head. I had made up a list. . . . that they would do all the things I did at home for him. You'd think I was putting him in a private home with a private nurse! I worried so, that he wouldn't be able to sleep or eat there. I even went to Dr. Samsel about baby food. I was afraid he would die; he was thin when he started.

Another mother recalled similar worries, whether there would be personal care for her child:

> Well, the food—if she would eat, if she would like the change of food. Nights if she went to bed if she'd have trouble sleeping, if she would cry and call for me. If they would have that attention like they'd have at home. She liked to eat, and would be eating between meals at home. . . . I worried a little, but I always had my friend to fall back on. She would reassure me, comfort me in any doubt I had. That sort of helped a little. We were told that she would get good care, and we know she does.

And yet, commitment had an irrevocability about it for those parents who could stop to reflect that now their claim to this child and his claim to them was technically at an end. Of their legal responsibility there remained an obligation to pay the assessed charges for his maintenance and, if need be, his funeral expenses. Such moral obligation as might continue was left to the individual family to determine. This problem would remain with them, but from now on the primary share of the responsibility for their child would rest with the state.

Parents vividly recalled the events of that day when finally they placed their child at the state training school. It marked a crisis as poignant as that earlier day when discovery had been complete. Some tried to control the events and plan positive things. One father recalled:

> I came home from work, and we got him ready; I sat them all down on the couch and took their picture. It was hard, but the picture worked out so well we used it the next Christmas.

Some families tried to give to the day of separation an air of "going away to boarding school." The child was outfitted with a new suit and clothing to wear at his new school. He was given to understand that now he, like his brothers and sisters, would be going to school—but a special school. One middle-grade boy who had been taken to visit a cousin at college accepted very well that he, too, was going away to college. The Southbury Training School looked like a college campus.

One couple with an insight into what would be best for their family gave their moderately retarded daughter a gala going-away party:

> [*Husband*] There were about a hundred people there, like a shower, so many presents and money. People had been so nice to her; they all wanted to see her before she left; and they came to the party. [*Wife*] And how they came!

Yet, for all the families who had kept their retarded child at home through years of struggle and hopes foregone, their reactions on the day they placed him at the training school were pretty bleak. A sensitive couple described it:

> [*Husband*] We realized then that the separation was inevitable. [*Wife*] I looked at him through different eyes. I felt that we were going to lose the family, lose Rolfe as an individual. He is endearing, playful, and has loving ways. You knew he loved you. He would never again have that kind of affection in his life. [*Husband*] The worst day of our lives. We drove up with another parent who was to visit. I had a long interview with the doctor in attendance—a regular work-up with a visiting physician sitting in. The worst was the actual parting when Mrs. Pitts put him in her car and drove him off to 32. She is vital to that day. We got in our car. It was a long time before we could drive home. I felt I had given him up, with this profound separation. If I woke at night I wondered what he was doing.

In most instances, both mother and father went, sometimes accompanied by a supportive friend or relative, sometimes bringing the other children too. Years later they could still remember the minute details of this trip along "Heartbreak Road," as one father called it; they recalled their feelings of shame and sorrow at what they had come to do. These separation pangs were sharp whether the retarded child blithely took it as a holiday jaunt, or had some premonition of the meaning of this journey. Some of the children had no reaction until the moment when their parents left them at the day's end.

Although the journey was short, the day's procedure was long. After reporting to the administrative offices the family then went to the hospital. The physicians gave the child a physical examination, which might be rather brief unless there were clinical symptoms that were unusual and interesting. Quite often these doctors had observed the retarded child before in their service to the out-patient clinic in the city.

A very ill child might then be brought to his assigned hospital-type cottage; but most of these severely retarded children remained waiting with their parents at the hospital while the mother and father by turn once more gave the history to an interested young intern. With a hyperactive or convulsive child this part of the process was tedious, burdensome, and somehow a letdown; but they learned firsthand of the hospital, a very fine one for research and remarkable for patient care. The chances were that their child would be a frequent visitor there during the ensuing year.

By midafternoon the business with the hospital was done; and now in the company of a supervisor the family drove to the cottage where their child would be a resident. If this cottage was in the children's village where the more capable children lived and the retarded child and his family oriented toward this change, the fiction of going away to boarding school could be maintained and the leave-taking tempered accordingly.

Said a father:

> Sure, I remember all the details. It was just a week before his eighth birthday. We had decided not to tell Richie about Southbury until the day we took him up there. We told him he was going to go to a great big school, bigger than the other children go to; he was being promoted, he had done so well at the ARC school. He was happy about it.
>
> We took him up to the cottage. As I recall, no fussing about our leaving him there. We left without staying with him. I think my wife was naturally upset, like having a child going away to school. I do not think either of us felt so much that we were leaving him at an institution as that we were leaving him at school. The kids were all running around happy, and the wonderful impression that a person like Mrs. Lloyd makes!
>
> There wasn't any acute sense of unhappiness or distress on the way back home. There was a very normal reaction. I think my wife had a little rough time about it, but there again, the usual thing that parents get when their child goes away to school. No, definitely not! I am positive neither of us did feel that we had given him up.

Another family had carefully prepared for this day and had good help getting through the experience:

> [*Wife*] The night before, all the family was over. They all brought her gifts. They all came over to see her.
>
> My friends came with us up to Southbury. We were pretty well in contact with them right along through that time. Clara ran right off in the cottage and started playing with the children; we called and she did not come back to us. She took a book and sat down. I had tried to talk with her right along—she was going to school, she was going to write and to color.
>
> [*Husband*] She went right into the new 7A cottage. [*Wife*] That gave me a lift, that she was going into a new cottage. In fact, Mrs. Locke was a nurse in the cottage where my girl friend's daughter had been before she became housemother of 7A; so my friend had told me how wonderful she was. We called Clara over and told her we were leaving and kissed her; but she didn't cry. [*Husband*] She saw all the kids, she was pleased. [*Wife*] Then Mrs. Locke told us as long as she was all right, maybe we had better go. The longer we stayed, the harder it was. We had stood around. In fact Mrs. Locke cried more than we did; she felt bad; she always does; she loves the children so much.

If this was an infirm and profoundly retarded child whom the parents brought into a hospital-type cottage, they might take immediate reassurance at seeing their child made comfortable:

There was the most ecstatic smile on her face when finally at the cottage they undressed her and put her in her crib.

Moreover, if there had been a desperate previous placement, the parents experienced positive relief. Already accustomed to the sad status of the children, including their own, their eyes would see only the evidences of efficient and tender care and intelligent concern. One wife remembered:

It was so cheerful; it was so clean. I liked the whole setup right from the start. I was quite impressed with the place; it made me think of the University of Maryland. She is as clean when I come on nonvisiting days. (My husband was planning on taking her from Marlowe over to Southbury. I got together with his mother, and we talked him out of it. I did not want him to see her for two or three weeks when she might have gained a little.) The place itself was all decorated for Christmas; it was terrific.

I was quite impressed with the people. This Dr. Lolli interviewed me. She asked all the questions that I considered important: Did she respond to affection? How about her feeding? Any special knack? I told her about the mirror I had put up near where I fed her. She would look at herself in the mirror; she would sit more still so that I could feed her more easily. The social worker also had been similarly interested when she called the year before.

We were permitted to take her to the cottage. We went back there after the afternoon interview with the doctor. She had had a good lunch, was comfortable; her toys were strung on her crib. (There were huge beautiful bouquets of flowers in the lobby and on the staircase at Marlowe; they had an aquarium and a nice circular drive; but, oh, those back rooms!) I was much relieved. I was relaxed emotionally for the first time in months. I felt she had to improve. I came home and described the place in glowing terms.

If, however, it was way back to a custodial cottage on the hill (where the lowest level children were cared for) that a family must bring a healthy trainable (but hyperactive) child, it was much harder. If this was a child who related to his family and took for granted his belonging with them, it was hardest of all—to leave him in the malodorous confusion of a crowded dayroom with other children whose condition and behavior and stigmata were so abysmally pathetic. There was dedicated care there also, parents did come to appreciate this; but on this first day the barren environment and the sad aggregate of children—blind, deformed, and incontinent—was too much of a shock, especially for those parents who had received no previous orientation. One mother described how it was:

I took my friend Lois because I had to have someone. Daniel walked right away from me and went to pushing a chair across the floor. I remember going into the dayroom and seeing all those children. It was so barren. And all those naked kids running around. And my Daniel came up there all dressed up, long pants and a blazer. I had brought up $50 worth of clothes and they had no clothes on. I burst out crying. I wanted to take him out of there fast. Mrs. Pitts physically ejected me; she put her arm around me and took me right out of the building. Lois was very helpful; she kept agreeing with Mrs. Pitts. [This mother soon was doing positive forceful things to help this cottage.]

Only rarely did such a child leave his parents and go into the dayroom, pick up a ball and commence to play among the other children. More often, the retarded child clung to his parents and had to be taken from them; or they were advised to leave by stealth, which added to their feeling that they were abandoning their child. There wasn't any easy way of leave-taking. This account from a father conveys the stress involved. His was a hyperactive boy perhaps mistakenly placed in an open cottage in the village:

It was an unusually warm day, June—June 5; I'll never forget that day as long as I live. Everything went along pretty smoothly until we were ready to go, and Andrew sensed that something was radically wrong. He had been amused and gay with all the new toys. Now he started to cry; we started to cry. That was the tough part of it. The lady who was in charge of the cottage finally locked him in a room. He put up quite a fight. We drove off. We felt very bad for weeks and months.

In some cases both parents went home and collapsed in grief and exhaustion. A few mothers and at least one father remained in bed for a week. Even parents with other children to occupy their attention went home to an "empty house." A couple described this interlude:

[*Husband*] We used to sit around the table, the three of us now—Carlotta's vacant chair there and then no eating for us. We felt better when we realized she was happy at Southbury. [*Wife*] There was a worn spot on the living room rug where she had sat all day in front of the television. When I used to be working in the kitchen I would look up and see her there. Now I could not bear it to look toward the living room.

The other children in these families, if they had not been properly prepared, would bear the mark of this commitment day. One family summed up their experience:

[*Wife*] We went right up to the cottage. It was probably the worst mistake we ever made to show Bernard into the cottage. Dr. Samsel was disgusted that we had been advised to bring him. [*Husband*] Maybe he shouldn't have gone into the cottage. I was very depressed when I went inside and saw some of the children there. And then on the way home my wife started to break down after putting up with it for years so well. After we got home she took to her bed for about five days. She really broke down.

Bernard was very lonely. He missed Ruth. He was in first grade then. Soon after that we were advised to seek assistance at the Child Study Center for Bernard. Dr. Robinson thought it would be a good idea for Bernard to be studied; we had switched to him as pediatrician. We had some interviews set up for Bernard and ourselves with Dr. Loeb, a woman psychiatrist. This was maybe two months after Ruth went to Southbury.

The events and feelings of this day of commitment were qualitatively somewhat different for those few families who had already made some satisfactory prior placement of their child in a private school or hospital. For them the real pangs had come with the first break; and this day simply marked going off to another school, where there would be permanent care and security.

Taking thought beforehand, some parents had made plans for the latter end of this day. A couple doggedly went through the ritual of a wedding anniversary dinner at a restaurant. One father stopped over in the city and took his wife and other children to a show, their first movie together in five years. The wife in this family described their activity thereafter until the first visit:

It was about three weeks. We tried to keep on the go, not sit home and brood. We alternated between visiting my sister and my girl friend. I had planned to clean the house after he left, but I didn't. I got out of the house, went to my girl friend's. She tried to keep me busy.

Several families took vacation trips immediately. Such a vacation usually a long-deferred one, did not hold much zest; but it was a constructive start on the different life the family would lead with the retarded child no longer in the home, and it also helped to pass the time until the first visit.

Three weeks' interim was the regulation. It was a wise rule and it was flexibly administered. Some very anxious parents were permitted to come sooner and to visit often without regard to the rules. This was apt to be the case where the child was severely and profoundly retarded, very infirm, and requiring constant nursing and medical care. Yet, these parents were the first to be reassured, sometimes at the very outset:

It was two days before the first visit. I had called as soon as I got home, and I called the next day, Wednesday; and Mrs. Pitts said I could come if I wanted to the next day. If I wanted to! Imagine! I went Thursday bright and early. . . . I felt much better after the first visit. They told me to bring back her hat and coat, and to bring back her dresses because they wanted to dress her. They had moved her room because they wanted to have her nearer the kitchen where they could see her all the time. She had no bruises, no broken bones. She was still in one piece and as pretty as ever.

Waiting longer at home, the fathers and mothers of healthier, more capable children suffered troubled days and "bumpy" nights until early visits to Southbury reassured them that all was well, that their child was already adjusting:

All we did was cry. We couldn't sleep, especially the first few nights. We just worried until we got to see her. . . . I called up every day. Mrs. Peters let Carlotta call me on the phone; she was asking so much for her mother. We had tried to prepare her: "You are going away to school and be a smart girl." She loved to mingle with people. Not afraid of strangers at all.

In a similar case, the parents recalled:

[*Wife*] We had been told that it should be two weeks, but—
[*Husband*] The week after, we got a letter she was sick in the hospital. We left Thanksgiving dinner untouched on the table and rushed up there.

[*Wife*] We went to the office and we spoke to Mrs. Peters, and she said it was all right. We had to get a pass, and she called from the office to the hospital.

When we got there, Clara was helping the nurses, taking all the pillowcases off the pillows. The nurses said, "Oh, we're having a grand time with her. We hate to have her go back to the cottage." They said they found her one time, she had climbed into bed with Margie, one of the house-girls at Cottage 7A who was sick at the same time. Margie got attached to Clara.

[*Husband*] There's a lot of good people in this world yet.

However, not all children of this level fared so well. For one girl, who had remained at home beyond ten, and who had a strong attachment to her family but little interaction with outsiders, adjustment to the new life was hard. Her mother recalled the tone of their first visit:

I felt terrible; she was crying; we were crying. You could see she hadn't been eating. . . . She was homesick and wouldn't eat. She didn't eat for a whole year. They tried to force-feed her.

There was a parallel case of an eight-year-old boy who had led a sheltered life at home. In this instance commitment had been especially hard, and the first visit proved distressful:

That was a tough day. Andrew wanted to come with us. They had to lock him in a room again. We felt just as bad, if not worse

> than the day we had brought him there. Andrew just clung to us. I thought he would rip my wife's dress. He never had spoken but a few words, but he found those words now, "Go home, go home," and he would go from one of us to the other, begging. We would try to leave, and then he would run after us. Finally, the house-mother said, "There is only one thing to do. I must take him and lock him in." To be honest, I felt so bad I thought, "I will take him back home again for a while, and we will think it over; then I will bring him back." Then I thought of the four years we had waited, and what would we do with him home again? . . .
>
> I kept saying to myself, "The child cannot be as helpless as they say, when he realizes he has a home and has this love for his parents and his home." If Andrew hadn't carried on the way he did, we might have felt he was not missing home so much. . . .
>
> This is where we made our big mistake. Our friends who drove us wanted to pick us up and take Andrew for a ride; but we were afraid he would think he was going home. So instead we hung around the cottage—it was two and a half hours of agony. He would drag us out of the place; we would walk around the grounds for a while. Every parked car he would open the door and try to get us in.
>
> This Cottage 20 was a little too advanced for Andrew, but he was also so very homesick that he wasn't cooperating with them at all. He was toilet trained at home, but up there he didn't even try.

This boy was then transferred briefly to a cottage on the hill where hyperactive children were protected in their difficult adjustment.

The more severely retarded, hyperactive children who had been assigned from the first to a custodial cottage had a somewhat different reaction. Their parents found them somber and unresponsive at their first and several subsequent visits. They conveyed to their parents their unhappiness.

One father felt:

> It almost seems like you had left him alone in the ocean in a rowboat. That is how they look at you when you come back to visit.

A mother pictured it:

> Rolfe was just a pair of ears with hands on him. He was withdrawn. He gave no sign of recognition or of pleasure.

These parents now feared that they had alienated their child emotionally, deprived him of the only strong basis for security he had. They were tempted to go up to Southbury and bring him back home.

The homesickness of these children and the suffering of their parents continued acute for several months. The parents' worry was augmented by the fact that a child who had been isolated at home was now apt to catch every children's disease and be frequently ill during his entire first year at the training school. Some parents did begin their acceptance of the training school for their child through their hospital visits with him during this first year; at the hospital they saw ample evidence of attention to the welfare and comfort of the children.

By the end of a full year most children had made real progress toward adjustment, even the hyperactive children in the custodial cottages. Meanwhile, the more capable of these were transferred to cottages in the village. In expressing their delight over this promotion to an open cottage, parents wanted to give full credit for the grooming the child had received. One couple expressed this:

> [*Wife*] The personnel in Cottage 32, Mrs. Pitts and the help, were wonderful. They kept it very clean, the way the children were. . . . Cottage 7A is out of this world! I hope he can stay there forever. . . . [*Husband*] As far as being social with the children, they were fine. From the first we considered Mrs. Pitts and Mr. Pitts the best; he called him Daddy Pitts; and the nurses were nice too. He got even more loving and care up at 32, because he was a little superior and they made a fuss over him.

Chapter 8

Readjustments and New Roles

As families realized that their retarded child was adjusting at Southbury, they could begin to restructure their lives at home. They needed to build themselves up again physically and emotionally. They needed to get operating efficiently as a household and functioning more effectively as a family group. They had to make a place for themselves once more in the social system of the community. (Since the retarded child's problem, they had been outside the culture.)

The parents were not enthusiastic about this new beginning. They were fatigued, and inertia that carried over from the last months of the waiting period still affected them. Behavior that had taken account of the retarded child in the home tended to persist. But nonetheless changes were made in response to demands.

They would have to attend to family health needs first of all. Often a major operation was needed. Mothers, especially, had neglected their health. Two fathers and several mothers were on the verge of a nervous breakdown. Sometimes one of the other children was suffering a severe emotional difficulty. Coping with these serious health problems gave an impetus to make immediate changes.

Families in sturdier health set about making little tangible changes in the household arrangements and routines. Usually the mother took the initiative. This was in her province, and she now had a couple of hours more a day. Most mothers did a thorough housecleaning, put things back where they belonged, rearranged the furniture. They got broken things repaired or replaced them.

The retarded child's room and play corner came in for constructive attention. The toys were sorted out carefully, the favorite ones put away against a happier day when he might enjoy them on a home visit. (Families with an infirm child put away his crib and disposed of his special furniture and appliances.) The parents refurbished the child's room, patched the plaster, painted, put up new curtains and shades. Some other use would be made of this room now. It might be assigned to one of the other children, perhaps to be shared with the retarded child on vacations from Southbury.

The family might also plan new major purchases, living room furniture, appliances to replace the battered ones. The husband looked for a newer car, "a better car so as to get to Southbury."

At the same time, they were revising the household schedule to fit better the needs of the family. They changed meal hours, the children's bedtime. They reassigned chores. The mother would have more time to spend with the other children. She could read to them, take walks with them. She could let them have their friends in to play after school, or even "have kids sleep over."

One mother brought a foster child into the home to provide companionship for her younger daughter. Also, a few parents sought to adopt a child to fill out their families.

Almost always physicians or other counselors had advocated having more children. Placement of the retarded child enhanced this prospect. And subsequent children, deferred for whatever complex of causes, now were born to younger vigorous parents. However, there was apt to be quite an age gap among the children born to these families, so their structure was permanently different from the norm.

A few mothers went back to school to qualify for a vocational career. Several mothers went out to work to get away from a lonesome house. Now the father would readjust his work patterns. He might work harder and for longer hours to compensate for a neglect of his job while the problem of the retarded child at home had been acute. He, too, might resume his education, go to evening college or foreman's classes. On the other hand, he might change his work schedule, or his job, so as to spend more time at home with his family.

There would be many more activities that the whole family could participate in, things the parents could share with the other children now. They usually began by planning short day trips or similar impersonal activities.

One young father commented:

> One week we get to go to the airport. Then you have to bring them to the zoo. We are living now. We are doing things as a family, as a unit, that we have never done before.

Another father said:

> Now we take the girls on weekends to Long Island, long day trips to the Bronx Zoo, that Circle Line trip around Manhattan.

These brothers and sisters had considerable adjustment to make after the retarded one went away. Much older children (and those born after commitment) were less affected. Often, though, there remained a psychological burden on the others. Children close in age to the retarded usually felt a strong attachment for him and had ambivalent feelings about his commitment. A younger one who related warmly to the retarded child just could not understand the separation, felt his own security threatened. In describing commitment day, a couple volunteered:

> [*Wife*] Mike was very attached to her. He couldn't understand it. . . . All the way home he kept asking, "Why isn't Sheila with us?" . . . He was three years old; it was an emotional shock to him. We had a time with Mike when she went. Mike would jump for the car; he wouldn't be left anywhere like Sheila! . . . [*Husband*] I had to threaten that I was going to get another pal before he would go to kindergarten. [*Wife*] He got on the bus to go to kindergarten. I can still see his pale, strained face when he was getting on that bus. . . . He is just coming out of it now; he is very shy at eight years old, and hates women.

A child who had assumed an especial responsibility for the retarded child was affected the most; he would grieve over his absence, be uneasy over the gap it made. Yet he would realize the necessity for commitment. He had borne the burden of the problem outside the home. It may have fallen to his lot to protect the retarded child in the neighborhood, to defend him from the children's slurs, and to explain him to strangers. Even in a tolerant neighborhood he would have been teased, or embarrassed by the retarded one's behavior. He might have developed an effective way of handling all this, but at some cost to his own social relationships. Such a child needed strong, affectionate support in adapting to the new circumstances in the family's life. Wiser, more sensitive parents were aware of this and tried especially to help him.

In any case, after commitment the pressure was off most of the children in their relations outside the home. They would like school a little better now and might do better work. They would enjoy doing things out in the community.

A fortunate father described his daughter's responsible role and continuing good social adjustment:

> At the present time, our daughter Mary has many friends, is quite popular at school. She is president of her sorority. All the sororities, all five of them, wanted Mary. Her marks also are very good. They have already asked her to be a candidate for the Queen.
>
> On her own, Christmas time she went into Lerner's without saying a word about it to apply for a job. The manager said, "We could use a girl with your appearance and personality. Go get your working papers and report tomorrow."
>
> As far as I can see, it has had no marked serious effect on Mary. Occasionally, when Andrew was still at home pestering her, she

would get upset. My wife and I today are amazed after what Mary went through with Andrew that she has turned out so well. . . .

Mary always loved her brother very much. Before he went to Southbury, she once said that she would not love Andrew any greater if he were a normal boy. Mary willingly sacrificed quite a lot for her brother. My wife would urge her to go to the Saturday movie with friends, but she'd say, "I would rather stay home with Andrew." I want to make it very clear to you that my wife never compelled her to take care of Andrew. Maybe all this made her the fine person that she is—her responsibility and strong feeling for the family. Even when young she sensed that it was a burden to be shared by all of us in the family. . . .

Mary would not be having the life she has today—the work, the friends, the success and popularity at school, the kids coming over to our house. Andrew at home would have reached a point where he would have been uncontrollable.

The adaptation of the children at home to the new family structure and the acceptance by the retarded child of his role at the training school would foster the parents' progress toward readjustment. Readjustment for the couple was slower than for the siblings. It took even longer if there had been disagreement * over what to do about the retarded child.

This entire problem made for an intense husband-wife relationship. A couple would affect each other's moods and capacity to act, throw each other off the track of effective functioning. When one of them was upset, this was communicated to the other. (Some of the constructive things they tried together soon after commitment seemed to be failures. The vacation trip they planned may have been an uneasy, unhappy time. The family's first attempt at providing temporary foster care may have proved discouraging.)

But equally, this sensitivity to each other meant that a couple could understand one another's feelings, andticipate one another's reactions, and offer a solace that wouldn't arise from a less involved relationship. A husband said:

Yes, yes, we did feel that we had given him up. You have a son and then you don't. She did feel that too, but she was smart enough not to let on to me. She was trying to comfort me, and I was doing the same for her; but I guess we had the same thoughts running through our minds, the same feeling.

A wife remembered:

My husband would say in the middle of the night, "All right, we will go up in the morning and bring him back home." That would ease me. If it hadn't been Southbury, I am not quite sure I could have left him there.

* These families in the sample were all intact, although there had been two instances of temporary separation before commitment.

When a couple had quite approved of one another's behavior under the stress of the problem, their attitudes were positive:

> [*Husband*] I am rather proud of both of us, that we worked this together. We weathered it a lot better than some do. I think when they blame each other, that's what separates them. [*Wife*] We never blamed each other. [*Husband*] If we have something to say, we get it out and do not mull it over.

The positive feelings came more slowly for some others. It was physically possible to have dialogue now, if they were on good enough terms to talk with one another. They could discuss their thoughts and concerns at night after the children were in bed; they could convey how they felt. And as they became reconciled to how things were working out, they would feel more relaxed toward each other and might develop a warm relationship again.

Couples did have more time to devote to each other's needs. They would try to plan little special occasions for each other and the family:

> We'd like to have more dates, my wife and I: concerts, plays, out to dinner as a family group.

They might enjoy just staying home together:

> [*Wife*] We do not go out much even now. [*Husband*] We feel free to, whether we do or not. [*Wife*] Yes. [*Husband*] Just climb in the car and go visit someone—that is new to us. [*Wife*] We get a babysitter easier. [*Husband*] Just to be able to read the paper through or watch a television show all the way through, or to have a meal in peace.

They would begin to do more socially, but at first with just a few selected people. Some had found another couple with a similar problem. Some had friends who related warmly to their retarded child, or relatives who had been especially supportive. They would concentrate on such emphathic relationships during this period.

As time passed, they would begin to entertain. Together they would do informal visiting with other friends and neighbors. One gregarious young couple quickly resumed a very active social life.

> [*Husband*] It has allowed us both to do a lot of things that were more difficult before. We could not rope in the neighbors to sit before, although there was a lot of exchanging. We got out sailing four or five times this summer. Before, my wife would have to stay ashore with Ruth. . . .
>
> Some of the neighbors actually envy how we get as much fun out of life as we can. Most of our neighbors are professional people with more money. Just in our own way, we set a pace with many of the couples that are in our own age group. We do things, horse

around a little. We just try to squeeze out as much fun as possible. There is a lot of fun in life, and it doesn't all tie in with money. One of these days I'd like to invest in a good phonograph and let Bernard discover Bach and Mozart. I studied classical guitar.

After a year or so, parents might deliberately try to widen their social boundaries through increased participation in family-oriented activities at the church, lodge, social club, or PTA. The activities they provided for the children at home came to resemble what was common in the culture. Upon their children's behalf, they took part in the organized projects of the community. If they were reluctant (and there was a tendency among these parents to want to keep their involvement in the community rather tentative), their other children, younger ones usually, brought them out. One mother said:

It had made a difference as far as making new friends. I have become very active; I became a scout leader right after she went away—PTA, Sunday School.

During this whole period after commitment, many families had discussed plans about moving. Concerned friends often made this recommendation. The house itself might for some time have been inadequate for the family's needs, the neighbors been indifferent, and the neighborhood changed. However, even with all these debit factors it didn't pay to move precipitately; this would be an ineffectual running away. Those families fared better who accomplished the beginning of their readjustment in the old home, perhaps even brought their child from Southbury for his first visits there, who got used to the emptiness there, let time wear things off a little.

In a year or so several families carefully planned a move to a new house, searching out a location that would fit the changing needs of their family. It might be nearer congenial friends, a place where there would be more social activity for the children, or better educational opportunity, a place closer to Southbury, perhaps a place with space and privacy suitable for having the retarded child home on occasion.

The most fundamental change after commitment was the redefining of the family role of the child away at the training school. This retarded child had been the focus of attention at home, the center about which all household activities revolved. He might have been the dominant figure in an isolated household, a strange monarchy ruled by its weakest member. While at home, he had established an almost exclusive claim to his mother's time and energy.

These families, good capable parents, could not "put their retarded child away and forget about him." They could not close out their relationship with this special child. It took some time, though, for them to realize the changed situation after placement, to accept that all their relations with the retarded child would be mediated by the training school now. Their major contribution to his adjustment, their main part in their child's life would be their visits to him and where feasible his home visits with them. But this would comprise a small portion of the hours of his life.

The training school encouraged visiting. There were two afternoons each week when families might come—and the first and third Saturdays and Sundays of each month were visiting days. One couple put it this way:

> [*Husband*] I think they stress the point you visit them. They do not like it when the parents stay away. They do not want them to be forgotten children. [*Wife*] There have been cases where the parents have been away so long, children didn't recognize them. The nurses don't like it.

Even with very severely retarded children, it was better for parents to visit. If a child was able to walk, they might take him for short walks on the grounds. They could bring him to the canteen at "Main Street," but a quiet, leisurely ride, with snacks in the car, might work out better.

Parents also might take an infirm child for a short ride, if they could manage to lift him into the car. In very nice weather they might take him outside for a walk in the wheelchair, or bring him to the school picnic grounds where he could lie on a blanket. As these children grew older, and perhaps feebler, it might be better to visit them on the sun porch at the cottage. When there was no recognition of them as parents, they might still come, with decreasing frequency, just to be sure that their child was receiving adequate care. Most of these infirm children had never been home after commitment.

Some families did try home visits with children below the trainable level whose health permitted; but they would find these less rewarding than visits in the sheltered environment at the training school, where there was ready help and acceptance of the child's behavior.

Even when parents continued unhappy over their child's placement in a low-level custodial cottage, to stay away completely might compound their suffering. Even if they could get little comfort from the visit, their child might. And if he didn't, and couldn't relate to them, they could still do positive things for him and the other children—custodial cottages always need help. They could work to improve things; they could contact the right officials with suggestions, not just go to the cottage charge with complaints.

Parents could bring gifts, carefully chosen toys and play equipment for all the children. Some parents who wanted to feel they were keeping a close contact with their child helped to start a quasi-PTA at his cottage. They held bake sales and rummage sales down at the school. They bought a canopy for the play-yard, a high-fidelity music system for the cottage. They took part in the big projects of the Home and School Association, like the drive to get a swimming pool for Southbury, whether their own child could benefit or not.

When a mother was worried over a health problem of her child, she could go to the head of the medical services. If certain routines or policies at the cottage distressed her, she could get an explanation from someone in authority:

> I had quite a talk with Dr. Samsel about the shoes. He told me, "You're saying that you would not want to walk around barefooted or to sit on a bare floor. These children are not going to mind. They do not care whether they have shoes on. Your boy might wear shoes, but the kid next to him would take his shoes off and hit him over the head with them! And as for more clothes, one half throw their pants over the fence and the other half wet them."

In the course of this discussion she learned that the children were trained to discard wet pants, the sooner to get a replacement pair, and that they were dressed lightly so as to harden them against colds.

Gradually, as she kept in touch, a mother might come to appreciate the care her child received, and be relieved of her anxiety:

> They have put him on a routine; he eats well. He seems happy. They take care of him physically, keep him dry, warm, and well. I think they have done all that any institution could offer. . . . When I saw some of the other children, I was glad that if I had to have a defective child that he was what he was—a pleasant child.

A mother in keeping contact with her own child might venture further (and help to implement the Southbury Training School visiting policy):

> I knew the parents of this boy in Cottage 26. He never had any visitors for they never went up to visit him. I asked the Cottage Life people if I might take him out, and they said yes, if I didn't take him off the grounds. So I did. He enjoyed it so much. He got in the car and had the radio on; he waved to all the kids. I had wondered if the child would benefit from going to ride.
>
> I waited eight months before I got an opportunity to tell his mother that I had been going to see him. She cried, but she said, "That is just the push I needed." She went up for the first time in ten years this Christmas. That boy who hadn't seen his famly in ten years remembered his sisters' names and all.
>
> This boy is in Cottage 26; and he is still so elated that he has me for a visitor. Now he hugs me when I come. The cottage parents are very nice there. . . . My Daniel will go back into the cottage willingly if we leave the other boy at his cottage first.

These boys benefited from the visits. There was a wide range in capability among those children who could. If their health was adequate to handle the strains and stimuli of a visit, if they could respond to their families' attention, it was worthwhile. Many parents kept a steady visiting contact, looking for no other reward than a happy smile from their child.

One father observed:

> I've been to Southbury so much I can just put the car on the road and hit it. We even went after the hurricane, when we had to go around by Bridgeport.

A mother said:

> We missed only once in twelve years, and then we asked a neighbor to go up and visit.

Families soon learned that regular visits on the appointed Sundays or Saturdays were better than either more frequent or sporadic ones. They had better come on a Visiting Sunday if their retarded child was aware of the significance of this day at Southbury, and many middle-grade children were. This, then, would be the retarded one's day, when he would be at the center of the family—but he would be at the center for a brief time only. The other children in the family would soon realize this.

In the early years parents tended to take their retarded children off by themselves for a picnic. They took long rides and explored the surrounding countryside. Perhaps they prospected for a vacation homesite on some rural hillside—perhaps this was a game. "I know every cowpath from Danbury to Waterbury," said one father.

Others did not range so far afield. A mother of a trainable middle-grade child told of their routine:

> I like to get him out for at least a short ride; we take him to a roadside restaurant. One thing that kid loves, he'll eat any time of day. You figure there are some things he doesn't get, such as hot dogs. At home he would eat four hot dogs at a clip. He always looks in my pocketbook for gum. We stop over back of the Gate House and let the two of them play on the grass. He is content; he would just sit in the car and ride. He'll sit next to you and never a peep. He is just content to go with you.

But with the years, the nature of their regular visits to Southbury changed. They got accustomed to the place and to the children there. The facilities for visiting on the campus were greatly enlarged and improved. In addition to the "Main Street" canteen and the Gate House, a new recreation area was developed, with a large artificial lake, an athletic field, and a playground for younger children. This had long been a vision of the school's administrators; it became an actuality in the 1960's. A large picnic area for parents and friends was developed in the pine grove nearby.

Now parents might stay right on the school grounds throughout the long afternoon. They could make of this Southbury visit a gala day for all their children. The children could play ball, go wading in the brook, fish for perch in the lake. In early spring they could fly kites and in winter go skiing and tobogganing on the slopes in front of the Administration Building. The younger children and the retarded tagged along, or played on the swings and slides.

Brothers and sisters were welcome to enjoy the special activities at the training school. There was the annual Roselle School exhibition and open house, the Fourth of July parade, a summer fair and arts show, and the soapbox derby. The colorful tractor-powered "sight-seeing train" was on the road for every such occasion; all the children loved to ride it.

From spring through Indian summer families brought out their charcoal grills and coolers, their fried chicken and salads, and picnicked under the trees. They brought friends and made friends among the other families who visited regularly. Some hardy souls persisted until Thanksgiving; on bright fall Sundays they sought a south slope or the lee of a wall where they could enjoy their sandwiches. The retarded one's appetites knew no season.

Even in summer the "Main Street" canteen held a sociable throng, buying ice cream and visiting; on winter Sundays the families crowded in.

Imperceptibly, the parents had come to feel more comfortable and more at home at the training school. They became accustomed to the other children more afflicted than their own, could sympathize quietly with their families and help them feel comfortable and secure there.

For all but the very infirm, home visits had their value, too. Most families evolved a regular pattern for these: at Christmas time, the Easter season, a short week in summer during the father's vacation—and occasionally on that end-of-the-month fifth weekend. Some families had their child home more frequently, some less often. But even the rare one-day visit, a surprise for the mother's birthday, was good for family morale in the early years.

A child of quite modest capability could enjoy the remembered activity at home:

> First he sits down and cries for a while. Then he remembers the bookcase and takes all the books out and then he walks up and down the stairs continuously. We take him for a ride, visit friends who have known him since he was a baby. We take him for a walk around the circle there. We put out the playpool if it is summer.

"I would like him home once in a while," this mother said, "because I would like the boys to know he belongs here." Her little retarded boy may have derived similar reassurance.

Gradually, however, families did cut down on the frequency and duration of home vacations as their retarded child came to accept the training school as his second home. Most cottages provided a secure environment with the right balance of play and work activity, freedom and discipline. Some cottages guided by personnel with warmth and wisdom, developed into loyal high-morale groups with real fellowship and mutual help among the children.

Especially would the parents of a middle-grade child realize that he was enjoying the richer activities at Southbury. Now, in the ordinary course of events, he was going to church on Sunday, to the movies every week, the block dances on summer Sunday evenings. The training school marked all the holidays, even to having Santa come in a helicopter at Christmas. There were special excursions for him and his cottage mates to Black Rock State Park, to the rodeo at the New Haven Arena, even as far as the Bronx Zoo. Why bring him home so often to play alone?

Up at Southbury he went twice a week to the pool, perhaps learned how to swim. At home his parents no longer dared to take him to the beach because of the hazards and crowds. Up there he might have attained a place on the sheltered work detail, or have a little job in the cottage. There was no meaningful work for him at home.

Ultimately, parents came to feel that Southbury was his place and that their child realized he belonged there. As he identified with the school, as he accepted his life there, and as they continued to make a new life for the family at home, parents would become reconciled to having him at Southbury:

> The thing he is getting is the companionship he really wants. He has asked to go back to school. They have made him more contented. I don't say they have increased his thinking power, but at least they have given him companionship with other children his type. . . . One of the reasons we like Southbury is he is safe now.

> I think they have made him feel that he belongs. He is happy there. . . . He has become more independent in little personal ways. . . . The feeling of separation isn't as acute because we are better acquainted with the school.

> They make you feel she's still yours. They're just taking care of her for you.

> We feel that we are finally on the right track as a family. Our son is being helped; and at the same time we are being helped to lead a normal life.

I did not realize until recently when she is well and happy at Southbury what a great difference it had made in all our lives.

I'd say there were two kinds of happiness. In a way, yes, we are more happy; we are leading a much more normal life. The children are leading a better life socially. And yet we are not happy that she has to be out of our home, that we have to have a child in that condition.

More peace of mind I think I have.

The day he walked into the cottage by himself, the first time he didn't cry I felt so good. I went home and had the first good sleep I had had since he went up there. If he would just say, "Mommy," that is what I pray for. He laughs like any other child and can cry, but he has no speech. He is so glad to see me when I come, puts his arms around me and hugs me.

Section II

Three Family Profiles

Family Profile I

In this American family, the parents were in their late forties. They were an attractive, dignified couple, quite influential in the community; they seemed to be of above average intelligence, social-cultural background, and education. The husband had had one year of college, then withdrew at his father's death. The wife was a junior college graduate. The husband was a salaried employee at an industrial plant, a skilled operator. The husband was an agreeable man, "an old-fashioned father" who left the problems of the home and children to his wife. He was a good steady provider, though. The wife was a highly intelligent, quite sensitive woman. She seemed to have a strong but gentle character, and considerable missionary zeal. If the problem of retarded children had not claimed her attention, this woman would have worked equally in some other worthy cause. Both the parents were quite active in church work. The family was staunch Protestant.

They owned an older two-family frame house located in an older section of the city. A close relative occupied the second floor apartment. The home was in good repair; the housekeeping was excellent. The furniture though not new was of good quality.

There were four children in this family. A girl twenty-three had attended college for a year, having won a scholarship; she had left school to be married. A boy twenty-one was a college senior, who planned to attend law school. A girl three, "a very intelligent child," as yet had no educational plans.

The child away at the training school was an eight-year-old boy, who had remained at home until nearly five. Trainable to a minimum level, he had had affectionate care from his mother; but his continuing need for constant watching and his hyperactive behavior became too great a burden for her. After a rather rocky start in life, his health had been quite good. His mother had early suspected that this child was not right. He had been the product of a very difficult, and possibly negligent delivery; he came home from the hospital with a broken arm. But quickly it was apparent that he didn't have the reactions of a normal baby:

"He didn't even hold up his head; his head was bobbing for so long. . . . He was like a premature baby. I asked about him at the hospital, but the doctor at the hospital said, 'Give him time; he had a difficult birth.' "

When he was two months old, the day before Christmas, his mother found out that time wouldn't help:

"I called up Dr. Levin. I had an appointment just before Christmas at four o'clock. He told me that he would never develop normally. I said, 'Physically or mentally?' He said, 'I mean both. You come back sometime, and we'll talk about it. Didn't they tell you at the hospital? They should have told you.' . . . I never went back to Dr. Levin, even though he said to come back to talk about it. I would rather have known it from the beginning and learned to face it. One day you're in despair and the next day you're hoping.

The husband added:

"There are two kinds of reactions—the wife's and the father's. The father has both child and mother to worry about. She almost lost her mind when she found out about it, to the state that she was afraid of her own shadow."

The wife continued:

"Dr. Levin said he would be an idiot. I came straight upstairs, put him in his bassinet, sat on the side of the bed, and looked at him. . . . I don't think I slept that night. I had company coming for dinner. How was I going to get through that meal? The baby's godparents—should I still ask them? . . . People try to console you. If I had a hundred children, I would still feel the same. I had a still-born baby just the year before, so I wanted this little boy."

The mother's efforts to get professional help were frustrated at that stage by her own feelings. She called on a doctor, an old friend of the family. He was concerned and said to her, "You're too nervous to nurse a baby." The wife remembered: "That was at three months, but I didn't tell him what was wrong at that early time. I just couldn't. I wasn't ready. I started to; I wanted to; but I just couldn't bring myself to." Later this same doctor was to help her through the period of her son's going away to Southbury.

She also went early to the New Haven Hospital Clinic, but although the chief doctors examined her son, she was unable to cope with the brisk and impersonal treatment. She did not bring him back for a subsequent appointment. However, her inherent intelligence, her realization—"if you have any piece of machinery where there's a part missing, that is the way it is with him"—protected this family from the quest after miracle drugs and cures. Meanwhile they read everything so as to understand about retardation.

The wife answered that she was not comfortable in the beginning discussing her son's problem:

"No, not too much. It put a strain on. He wasn't a child you could take places and visit with. I remember this friend asked me, 'Why doesn't he sit up? When is he going to sit up?' when he was nine months old. Not until he was a year old did I begin to tell people that he was retarded. Wesley came between a good friend and me. I didn't try to hide him. There were times we felt like doing it. Once we were out riding; we came back and were going in the house, when I saw a woman I knew coming down the street. I made myself stand and wait when I saw her coming; and I greeted her with him beside me. One woman came to see me just once—out of curiosity—just to see him. We met her and were gracious. She said, 'Would he talk? I suppose he talks when nobody is here.' . . . It got easier to talk, after I joined the parents' association—when I understood how many people were in the same boat."

Another pregnancy was out of the question:

"I told the doctor at the Child Study clinic maybe if I was ten years younger. . . . The little one just came; she wasn't planned. I guess God had something to do with it! She has done a lot for us. . . . This time I was in labor a very long time. The doctor said it was psychological, that I had gotten afraid to have the baby."

These older parents were sturdy, but the child "was very aggressive, hyperactive, and he was destructive." When the wife became pregnant again, she really couldn't handle him. He would run away. If her eye was off him, he would climb on the high secretary where the key was kept, then let himself out the front door and into the busy street. Sometimes neighbors brought him back; once a policeman retrieved him down the block. The child waked early, and he was difficult to settle at night. His mother would have to lie down with him until he would fall asleep, at nine or ten o'clock when it was too late to go anywhere. Only once did she leave him in the evening with her daughter "When he was in that bad stage"; she had a terrible time. To a question regarding advice from friends, the wife replied, "Nobody told me how to manage him. They wouldn't even attempt to tell you how to manage that boy!"

The husband recalled that he was most troubled by ". . . just the condition he was in, knowing we couldn't even hope or do anything for him!"

The older siblings did not appear to have sustained any lasting damage from this experience, but it must have been very hard for them during that early period when their mother was so considerably upset. There was a little pressure on them, coming more from curious adults in the neighborhood than from their high school mates; but these were very sturdy young people. Indeed, the mother recalled that they seemed better able to accept their retarded brother as he was then than they the parents:

"I never took pictures of him, but my daughter took lots of them. They accepted him as a baby more readily than I did. They took him out where I wouldn't . . . There was never a problem like that. The older children had strong affection for him. They were very good to him. *(smiling)* My son may have helped to make him a little rougher; he played rough-house with him."

This problem had a serious impact on the mother's health; and for some time her too complete preoccupation caused her to withdraw from even her close personal relationships:

"I sort of forgot about my other daughter and son—the stupor I was in. I was so wrapped up in Wesley. They came home from school and said, 'We're getting so we don't want to come home from high school any more now. You're so sad all the time.' I was just going and doing my work mechanically. I didn't talk and discuss with them. After my housework, I'd retire to the bedroom with Wesley.

"I had all kinds of weird thoughts, even suicide. I must have been emotionally unstable. It may seem ridiculous. One night my husband came in, and I just fell all to pieces. If he had taken me to a doctor or to the hospital, they would have sent me to Middletown. I knew Wesley was mentally retarded, but I hadn't accepted it."

Gradually the needs of her other children and husband and the claims of her friends drew her back toward her accustomed life. But despite the kindly attitude of friends and relatives toward the little boy and his trouble, she felt alone with it:

"I didn't feel I had *anybody* I could really talk to. I wanted somebody to talk to, but there wasn't anybody. I wasn't close to my mother. There wasn't even a minister's wife that I could go to who would help me. That first year I just felt, if I only had *somebody* to talk to."

It was really after she began to plan for her retarded son's future, after the parents enlisted the support and counsel of the physician who was a family friend, that the wife was able to resume a normal social life. She felt that her active participation in the new parents' group, the Association for Retarded Children, had been a help to her. A few years later the happy advent of the baby daughter had fostered her complete recovery.

All the time that this retarded child was at home, his presence affected the couple's social-recreation habits. When he was a young infant, it had been the mother's strong feelings about this trouble; later the little boy's hyperactive behavior was a barrier to social activity. Fortunately, the child was also quite appealing and generally happy and friendly. This family had owned their home in this neighborhood for many years, and were securely established in their social, church, and neighborhood relationships. This factor offset somewhat the parents' considerable sensitivity. The wife told how it was:

"We used to take people for rides with us. . . . I couldn't enjoy going in the car with him; he was so active in the car. I disliked Sundays more than ever because on Sundays everybody would be out with their babies and I couldn't go. . . . We couldn't go on picnics as we used to do, or do the things we did before. . . . We did keep playing cards with one couple who knew Wesley's condition. I did continue with my club and had it here. But I wasn't too happy about it. You sort of force yourself to, because you know you need to. I don't know how I got through those days. We couldn't go out together."

The husband interjected:

"No, because we felt we were social outcasts, because we had Wesley. I was out, and I never carried my problems onto my job. I had loved cards, but my principal friends drifted away, . . . There was no effect on my work. You kind of brace yourself. I didn't discuss my problem with the men at work."

The wife had been active in voluntary groups; this activity she continued, and became especially interested in efforts toward helping handicapped children. Her feelings about this whole problem bear quoting:

"It's a sort of sorrow that can stay with you, that you carry with you. It is a different sort of sorrow from a person dying; it can stay with you always. In the beginning, it possesses you and takes over all your personality. As time goes on, you push it into the background, but this is a constant sorrow."

The wife said, "I had been active in church. I curtailed it somewhat then, but now we both go regularly, and both of us are quite active." Earlier, the husband had remarked that after the retarded child's birth "My wife did more reading of the Bible the next year than she had ever done."

This husband was quick to say that their son had not occasioned them any "unusual expense, not a lot of doctors' expenses." Nor were there probably any indirect economic effects. On a modest salary he had managed well to put his older son through college and pay the Southbury assessment for the younger. He had no complaints.

The boy was three when the mother became convinced of the need to apply for Southbury. Guided by the family doctor, she had gone with him to a specialist and then to the Yale Child Study Center. At the Child Study Center they were thoughtful, told her about Southbury—"They said it had done wonderful work." It was the family doctor, however, who helped her most toward a decision:

"Dr. Nickels said it wasn't fair to myself to keep Wesley; that it wasn't fair for me not to lead a normal life; that there wasn't anything I could do for Wesley; that he would be happy there even though I wouldn't be happy having him there. He told me about a friend of his with a child like that, and what they did."

There was not much help from relatives and friends on this issue. One did advise they "put him there and forget about him," but most of them (who had never taken care of him) were against an institution for him, and urged the mother to continue with the fine care she was giving him.

For the wife especially this going-away period wasn't easy:

"When it got nearer the time for me to be separated from him, it was harder. I didn't want to. The hardest thing I had to do in my life was when I took him to that cottage, and I wanted to grab him and bring him home. Our friend said, 'Let's not say anything, just sneak him in the car and we'll go.' . . . I had known for a long time that he would ultimately have to go. It was only the feeling of having to put him there that bothered. Oh, that I could have kept him a little longer, so that he could have had more of the love."

She knew his care would be adequate, but she thought about:

"The little things he wouldn't get—his being warm enough, that extra bit of food that he might want. . . . They wouldn't have time to recognize his needs like I did. . . . I felt kind of lost that first week. My sister-in-law said, 'Let's just ride up there and try to see him.' "

She did not see him that day, which was perhaps just as well; the early visits for both mother and child proved terribly difficult:

"At first it was just Wesley's attitude. He sat on the floor with his legs folded, and didn't do anything. He wasn't active at all, didn't move, didn't play. I picked him up and put him in my lap, and no reaction and no interest. He wasn't interested in the toys. He cried when I left him; he pulled on me; that was the only sign."

The father could not bear to go up to the cottage.

In the years that followed, these parents had become boosters of the training school. The mother was a faithful committee worker. She had a high opinion of the staff, the program generally, but still grieved for her son in that "cottage forgotten up there on the hill." With a few other parents she had sought to stimulate interest in the plight of these "below-trainable" children, and to secure better facilities and program for them.

The husband was more reconciled. He saw the lack in terms of inadequate appropriations and insufficient personnel, and admitted that for his boy to have the training they would like for him would impose an expensive "per-patient ratio"—"for boys like ours they would need to have an attendant for about four kids." The husband was quick to say, "There are compensations":

"He has filled out; his health is good. The physical care is good. And he enjoys the companionship. He doesn't have to be prepared for anything. It's your own feelings about the place that bother you; Wesley likes it."

The wife did agree that their son had made a happy adjustment.

Because the little boy's hyperactivity had thus far made home visits impracticable, the parents had adopted the custom of entertaining in their home at holidays children from the training school who were "educable"—candidates for placement in the community. At the time of the interview they had with them such a girl, who had spent Thanksgiving week at their home.

The parents "still feel that Wesley needs us, though we don't know that he recognizes us as his parents." They had acted on that feeling, and had continued to visit more frequently than was the custom upon the hill. They were happy that the child was responding and had reached the point in his training where they could with pleasure and safety take him to the Gate House for ice cream or for a romp on the school grounds. They never missed a visiting Sunday; the car knew the way; and it was always full of friends and relatives or other parents, whom they wished to introduce to Southbury.

Family Profile II

In this Irish-American family, the husband was in his mid-forties, the wife her early forties. They seemed a warm-hearted, very sincere couple of above average intelligence, average social-cultural background, and above average education. The husband upon graduation from academic high school had gone to work for his present employer; but he went on to study engineering as a part-time evening college student for eight years. He was an earnest, hard-working man, not too tolerant and understandably a little bitter at the misfortunes that had attended their efforts to raise this large young family. The wife seemed very devout, patient, and courageous. Despite her not too robust health and the stress that she had suffered, she had a very attractive personality. Her gentle sense of humor matched her husband's rather mordant wit. She was a liberal arts college graduate. She then attended a university school of social work, secured a masters' degree, and worked in that field until after her marriage. The family was staunch Catholic.

They owned and occupied a rather new one-family frame house, of moderate value and in a fair state of repair. It was located in a new suburban neighborhood.

There were six children at home ranging in age from twelve down to a year and a half. The parents described these children as normal in health and intelligence; the two oldest were honor students in junior high school. The retarded child away at the training school was a girl of six, the fifth of seven children in this family. She had remained at home until about four years old, when her uncontrollable hyperactivity compelled her parents to place her in a private boarding home of the hospital type. She was severely retarded and suffered from multiple physical handicaps, as the result of a birth injury the parents had been told. She had survived infancy with the exceptional care the parents gave her, but since three her physical and nervous condition had grown progressively worse. Just before the little girl's fifth birthday a place was made available for her at Southbury Training School.

For this family the discovery was foreshadowed at birth. There had been trouble—the cord, a difficult delivery. The father noticed that "her whole right side was jumping." The doctor told him that the oxygen supply to the brain had been cut off, causing the convulsions. The mother sadly returned home without a child for the second time. (Her previous baby had been stricken with epidemic diarrhea on the day they were to leave the hospital.) When finally they brought this baby home at three weeks, they were told that she would be slower than the other children. This exceedingly mild warning was forgotten when at three months an examination and psychological testing showed nothing wrong. Despite the child's poor health and general slowness, the parents held false hopes until about two, when the visiting nurse urged them to return with the child to the Child Study Center.

Simultaneously, a young doctor, summoned to an emergency in their home on the recommendation of their pediatrician, ministered to the little girl through an especially bad convulsion; and then told the wife what she had to look forward to. This man's honesty and advice were appreciated.

"He said that it would be progressive and get worse; he was the first who ever told me. He said that she would never be able to go to school. I did resent our pediatrician's not telling me. You have to have some guidance to know what to do. He told me only not to expect the same from her as from the other children, but he led me to believe that she would just be slower; that her coordination would be poorer, that she would not grasp things or hold them. You have to have guidance, and he did not give it to me."

The wife recalled her feelings when realization came to them:

"I didn't know that it was quite that radical. You know what a slap in the face that is. It was terrific. I was just dissolved. . . . I still am very grateful to that visiting nurse who got me to take her for that second test. I knew she was bad, but I never thought that bad—maybe that we'd have to work with her, and that she would be in a slow group at school, but not that."

The husband recalled:

"My wife was high in the air when I would get home. I couldn't say the right thing to her. She thought that I was pretty reserved about it. But I have had so many setbacks; if I failed, I failed. It had to be done, and that's all there was to it. They wanted to ease the pain in telling us at the Child Study Center. I said, 'Tell me the truth. I can see what's happening now.' "

The husband described the several serious bad times they had with the little girl's convulsions, the mad dashes and the all-night stays with her in the emergency room at the hospital. She had to remain there for twelve days after one severe seizure. At the hospital the doctor told them that they might be able to take her in Southbury in six months or a year.

They had made application after the psychological examination when she was two and a half.

The family might have coped with her seizures; but her very wearing hyperactivity, her screaming, the dangerous hazard of her behavior upset the other children and wore down the parents. They recalled her destructiveness and their desperate effort to fit her into the family. The father commenced:

"What we did, we'd try to advise the older children not to touch her or do anything to her: 'Just tell us. If she would get a knife or turn on the gas jets, don't fight with her, call us.' She would go and tear up their homework. They could not have anything to keep it nice. She would throw all the shoes down the stairs. She would tear up their books. Electric trains, dolls, she would ruin."

They had to put locks on everything. The wife kept the kitchen table turned over on its side, so that the child could not jump on it. There could be no curtains in the house; she would pull them down and ruin them. "She would plug up the toilet. She took the heavy top off the toilet tank once and broke it. One day I had gotten a new set of dishes; she pulled the whole tray off the table and broke them."

The husband shook his head ruefully: "We had a nice home and good furniture when we were married and lived in that apartment. Now everything is falling to pieces."

But it was the continuous random hyperactivity and the screaming that troubled these parents most:

"She screamed for one whole weekend. I was almost frantic. The local doctor said that she might be affected at the full of the moon, and it was quite often at that time of the month. She slept very little. She'd sleep in the corner of the sofa. I'd pick her up and put her back in bed. Then she'd wake up, and she'd turn the radio on in the middle of the night. Then we'd take her back to bed again."

She upset the rest of the children. They couldn't have any of their possessions around. If they came home excited and pleased with their report cards, she would get excited too and scream and scream. Mealtimes were a problem; the husband remembered:

"We tried feeding her alone. She'd scream and throw everything against the wall. I would say, 'Everybody quiet!' when we'd all eat together, and the other children wouldn't make a sound, but she would still throw glasses and dishes."

These children became extra sensitive; they cried easily. The wife felt the parents "took it out on the other children because we were worn out with her."

The huband said that it never got to the point where the neighbor children teased the siblings. He had been concerned about that; so they kept strangers out of the play yard. Necessarily, this severely retarded child had to be kept isolated. The father built a stout fence and padlocked the gate.

The eldest daughter, then eight or nine, was very good with her retarded sister, and was able to take some care of her:

"Shirley was good with her. She was the only one of the children who was. She has a soft quiet way about her. I thought that at that early age, I shouldn't be depending on her so much. . . . The boys had little patience with her. It bothered the younger boy."

The husband pointed out though: "If she was sick, they would all be concerned. If they went for candy, they'd always bring her some. They would take her on little walks. They were affectionate."

For a time, the younger siblings did poorly in school, but that was before her commitment. The parents believed that there had been no permanent harm to the progress or personality of the other children.

This problem imposed limits and change on the wife's personal relationships, but not at all within their old-fashioned, very solid immediate family. Isolation is a comparative thing, and with a husband and seven children to care for this wife could not withdraw very far. The mere process of keeping the school contacts of the other children in repair kept her out in the community; and of course, there was church. There was certainly strong mutual support, moral support as well as physical assistance, between husband and wife—"We always had pretty good teamwork." However, the extended family all had concerns of their own, and contact with them was tenuous at best. When a new baby made its advent, the husband would take his vacation and care for the home and children; and the visiting nurse might come in and help. Beyond the family, the situation was similar to many other cases. Old friends would proffer warm invitations that they were not in a position to accept—"Come over some night, any time; bring the kids." But except for one neighbor nobody ever came around to help out.

The social-recreation pattern of the family while the little retarded girl was home differed markedly from the norm for large young families. The other children could not have their friends in to play, not even in the fenced-in back yard. Birthday parties, even within the family, had to be abandoned; the retarded one would wreck the festive table. The money that went for medical expense erased from the family budget the item of recreation. They did make excursions to the beach, though. The children all loved it, so they went frequently—on off days when there would be no crowd to excite the retarded child. On holidays they had picnics in their own back yard. The parents were making this up to the other children; the summer just past, the father, assigning the expense to perdition, had rented a bathhouse for the entire season.

The couple had rarely gone out for an evening while their retarded daughter was still at home. Because of her convulsions baby-sitters were out of the question; but there was a greater barrier to social activity—"We would get so physically exhausted, the lack of sleep and the hectic days; it was just a full-time job with her." The husband had an avocation, which brought a little extra income and also provided him recreation. Besides that, he went to his union meeting. One day a week he would take charge at home. "My wife," he said, "would go all day Saturday; go to a movie, shop, get her hair done. It was a set ritual; she would be leaving on the early morning bus, and stay until five."

The wife expressed her gratitude for this weekly holiday, and then remarked:

"Otherwise, I never got out at all except for church. . . .We always got there; that was our morale. We never missed Mass; . . . You have to have something to keep you together; I don't see how anyone could last if they didn't have the church." He added, "We never missed Mass unless we were so sick we couldn't move."

The husband was rather bitter as he talked over how this problem had affected the family's economic life. First, he felt that it may well have held him back, slowed his progress with the company despite his long seniority and stable record. During the two years when their problem was acute he couldn't be so prompt on the job; he would be late for work three times out of five; they couldn't depend on him; he would have to leave suddenly for an emergency at home or a trip with the retarded child to the hospital emergency room. He felt his immediate supervisor had not been very understanding. Ultimately, he had "gone to the top men." There he got some wise counsel and some practical help:

"I had to go to a high Mason, who helped me. I give him all the credit. You try to handle it through your own church agencies, and you get no sympathy and no help. If they haven't had the experience, they don't know." This very devout couple could still be critical of the attitude of their clergy, who had just said: "Go to the state institution for help."

Queried as to the effect this trouble had on his financial position, the husband exploded:

"Wrecked it, totally wrecked it. I almost had to give up my life insurance. I still am loaned up. It will be another eighteen months before we get out of debt. It was a big financial strain. I was practically at the end of my loaning ability. . . . Each year about September I would get the previous year's medical bill paid, and then it would start all over again. We let everything else go. You have to pick out the essentials to keep the roof over you. . . . I have had a general raise since. The only tension is the financial loan that keeps me concerned."

These parents had applied for Southbury when the little retarded girl was three, soon after her testing at the Child Study Center and six months after the sixth child had been born to the family. With another pregnancy, the need became even greater to place this convulsive, hyperactive little girl. The wife remembered:

"I was afraid I would lose the baby. I needed proper rest; I had the phlebitis. . . . The doctor kept telling me, 'Rest and proper diet.' I lost all my top teeth. We were really desperate, back against the wall.

"I made arrangements that if Marcia wasn't placed by the time the new baby was born, I would place the new baby in St. Anthony's Home. I had to—if she got jealous—I had to make some alternative plan. I had to face reality. I was getting so on the ragged edge myself; it's a wonder the baby is as good as she is. I was wondering if I would have a baby to place."

The parents used every resource; they wrote letters, appealed to everyone they could think of who might help them in the placing of the severely retarded child. There was no bed for her in Southbury; the new building that would house her and half a hundred other little cases on the emergency list was not yet complete.

Finally the parents managed a temporary placement in a hospital-type boarding home, with some financial assistance from the town. Nine months later the transfer to Southbury occurred, but for the parents, psychologically, this was the commitment. The wife spoke of it:

"The only thing that reassured me was that Dr. Guertin had told me that any kind person could take our place. Marcia didn't regard us in the same way as normal children do their parents. She would be content with anyone. After I digested that fact, I was more resigned. She was pretty happy up at Mary's Children's Home. That is a well-run place. She only took bed-patients, but she made an exception for Marcia. We had to bring her for a visit first. . . . [Did you hestitate?] Oh, no. From what Dr. Guertin said, it would be a lifetime proposition where she would never be able to earn a living. She would be tossed from one relative to another, or be a burden to her brothers and sisters after we go. The consolation now is that she will be cared for whether we were there or not."

These parents had "played the part to the children of her going away to a different kind of school. We worked our own selves into that same belief; that was all." They didn't feel they had given their retarded daughter up. They had been even more pleased with the facilities and the care at Southbury. They went regularly to see the little girl, taking turns; they didn't often attempt to take the other children; they realized they could provide their daughter at Southbury with more pleasure that way. Family picnics hadn't worked out; she had missed their individual attention; the excitement overstimulated her. They felt that she had accepted Southbury as the "place for her to be"; "She is happy with the group there. It's home." They would continue to build a reassuring and satisfactory, though minor relationship with this severely retarded daughter through the medium of their frequent Sunday visits.

Family Profile III

In this Polish-American family, the parents were in their late thirties. In their cultural outlook they seemed closer to the immigrant generation than to their second-generation peers. They were an industrious, conservative couple of above average intelligence, average social-cultural background, and limited education. The husband's parents had reemigrated to Poland when he was four years old; he returned to this country on the eve of the Second World War. He had not learned to speak or write English, but he had mastered an intricate operation at the factory where he had worked since his return to the United States. He was now training other workers for this job. As a youth in Poland he had had the equivalent of about four years of schooling by American standards. He seemed mild-mannered, rather inarticulate, but quite capable. His wife was quite matter-of-fact about his cultural handicap, and very proud of him as a provider and a husband. She rather prided herself on having conserved the old-style virtues in raising her family and managing her home. Hers was, however, an enlightened conservatism. She was a keen and clear-thinking woman, whose formal education had been cut short midway through high school because of economic pressures at home; "There were three younger brothers to get through school." Until her marriage she was a semi-skilled factory operative. She had returned to a factory job after her retarded child had been away some months at Southbury, because being alone in the house and not enough to do had troubled her. The family were staunch Roman Catholic, the wife especially devout. They owned a small two-family frame dwelling built around the time of the First World War, located in a stable lower middle-class neighborhood. The wife's parents lived downstairs. The house was in good repair; their apartment was adequately furnished; the housekeeping standards were excellent.

There were three children home, girls, thirteen, nearly ten, and eight years old. The child away at the training school was the twin of the youngest girl. His mother had cared for him at home until he had passed his fifth birthday, although he was very severely retarded and physically quite infirm. Blindness and cerebral palsy were among his afflictions. In this young family where the other children were often sick, the care of this very severely retarded and infirm child was a burden. The parents entertained no illusions. For this little boy the outlook was as bleak as his present condition. Yet, this mother had been quite reluctant to place her son at Southbury.

The wife's recollections of the discovery period were very clear:

"Jerry had pneumonia when he was six months old. He had been sitting before his sister. There had been nothing wrong previously. He came up with a temperature of 106.8 degrees. . . . Dr. DeLeito had care of them, both at the clinic and on home calls. I couldn't believe the temperature could go so high. I called the doctor at eight in the morning, and he came at 1 P.M. and had him sent immediately to the hospital.

"He remained two weeks in the hospital with an oxygen tent and penicillin. He looked all right when he came home but could no longer sit up. I thought I'd wait a couple of weeks. Then in September I took him to the Well-Baby Conference; I told Dr. DeLeito. He said, 'I find nothing wrong with the child, but I will make an appointment at the New Haven Hospital Pediatric Clinic.' We had all the tests made. We had to go back in three months in January. Dr. Samsel was there. He said he had a form of cerebral palsy. He told us there was no hope for him whatsoever. He recommended Southbury. He is just the opposite of spastic; he has no control at all.

"I didn't give Dr. Samsel my answer right away; the thought of parting with a child like that was very hard. We discussed it, and we decided it was necessary. God forbid, something should happen to either of us—the child would be left God knows to whom. . . . We still didn't give up hope; we still kept going to doctors, though, that people would tell us about.

"That winter all four of them had measles, and Jerry had a severe convulsion. I never had seen a convulsion; I thought he had died; he stiffened all up. I called Dr. DeLeito but he was out of town. So Dr. Naylor came, and told us not to blame ourselves in any way, not to be ashamed, that things like that happen regularly, regardless of race, money; that there was not any stigma to the family from it."

The thoughtful counsel of this substitute pediatrician reinforced her intentions; it was probably then that she followed through and completed the Southbury application. It had been hard to accept the necessity:

"We felt very bad about it, as any other parent would. We couldn't understand why it happened to a child in a family where they would have the right care and to the mother and father who had wanted him. Beautiful healthy children are left to run barefooted on the streets. We were both clean-living, and hard-working. My husband has never been out from drinking or laziness. We are just an average family and do not go out looking for entertainment. We had those three daughters, good children, nothing wrong with them, but this was a son which my husband and I wanted so badly. As good as girls are, they are always for the mother. We felt bad, our only son, that it should happen to a son which he had wanted so badly as a companion for years to come. It was just disappointment that he should turn out like that. By crying you do nothing for the child; you only hurt the ones at home. They deserve a life of their own. Because he is like this, they shouldn't be made to suffer for it."

It might have been a little late for another son:

"We never looked forward to any; if they came it would be expected and natural; neither did we try to keep away from normal living. But I believe that if I had become pregnant, it would be hard. We never discussed it in reference to him, even among ourselves."

Although they followed the advice of Dr. Samsel and the pediatrician and made application for Southbury, in the intervening years they went to a number of doctors and voluntary agencies. Occasionally, one would raise false hopes, would urge them to hold off a while on Southbury. Fortunately, this road led them to the Crippled Children's Association, where the doctor helped her to understand:

"There was nothing that would help him. He might be taught to sit up and to be toilet trained, but nothing else. And he just told me to bring Jerry to the clinic for massages, and just wait for our Southbury application. He told me point-blank; 'Do not spend your money. This child cannot be helped, except as Southbury can do it.' "

[She was grateful:] "And yet it took our little hopes and put it straight that that was the end of it. The others had all promised that there might be something."

The wife explained the procedure she followed in this four-year quest for medical help:

"Whenever I went for any consultation, I went alone; my husband never went with me or spoke to the doctor. My husband was never present. I did explain to him what the doctor said. Any contacts that I made with the doctor or as far as getting him into Southbury, I made myself. It was hard enough to get to understand it myself without my having to interpret to my husband. He would always say, 'You go.' Then after the children had gone to bed, and the work was done, then we would discuss what happened with me that day at the clinic, and what course of action should be taken.The children were never involved in any of this problem. We never discussed it, medical or otherwise, with the children."

It was rather difficult to evaluate the effect of the retarded child's behavior on the functioning of the home. When the interviewer asked: "What aspects of Jerry's trouble bothered you most back then?" it was necessary to probe for this answer from the wife:

"He was so good, so happy. He would eat, would sleep day and night. He would never fuss at being wet. It was just that we felt completely tied down those years. I would never even go to the store, for fear that something would happen to him.

"He never cried or screamed in any way. I don't believe he knows how to scream. He just whimpered. The only thing he did was bang his head on the back panel of the crib. Even after he left, my sister downstairs and I felt that we could hear the noise of the crib in the back room. He was always the last one to be fed; after the older children were out of the house, I would say to his twin, 'Come on and eat, and I'll go feed Little Brother.' At age five, I had to feed him holding him like a baby. Even after he was gone, I would think I had to go in his room and feed him. I would even start to go in the room.

"With us it was like an assembly line system. . . . My husband leaves at 6:30. I had the day organized; I washed every day, ironed once a week; what didn't have to be ironed wasn't ironed. We did the best we could to be cleaned up by dinner time. On the nice days we might go for a little walk, and my mother would come up from downstairs to sit with Jerry for a while. That was a blessing. Daytimes she didn't mind, but there was no care involved. . . . My brother and his wife, before they were married, came to sit with another couple. They couldn't find the diapers so they pinned a blanket on him one time! *(laughing)* They still joke about that. My sisters never sat because they were at the going-out-with-fellows age."

The wife talked quite freely when asked what effect this problem had on the siblings. She discussed her attractive little daughters, fondly, yet half-deprecatingly:

"Jessica, his twin, remembers very little; she doesn't remember him at home. She knows she has a brother. They have not seen him since he went to Southbury. She doesn't remember what he looks like. Catherine is very desirous of going to Southbury and wants to see him. She says, 'What is the use of going up there if we can't go in and see him?' She is an impressionable child; I wouldn't let her go in to see him. She tells tales and doesn't mind who her audience is. I wouldn't take her in and have her see the others. . . . Diane, the oldest girl, was affected by it most when he was home. She came home crying from school one day. The children had been teasing her because she had a blind brother. . . . She never had friends come to the house. They would want to know what was wrong with him—'Why doesn't he sit? Why doesn't he talk?'

"It is hard for me to have a conversation about this, especially to explain to children. Unless I am wound up, such as with you people, it is hard to tell."

The wife believed that the social life of the little girls had been unduly restricted while the retarded boy was at home. There seemed to be no continuous effect. The wife had not shared the burden with the little girls.

The wife had described briskly her own family background; this decription offered a clue to how she managed her personal relationships under the impact of this problem:

"My family were all well. My father and mother, married thirty-nine years, are still well and happy. No bills or financial worries ever—I was brought up through the depression, and we never knew what a depression was. My father always was the only one to work, and he always had work. My mother was a good manager at home. We had always been a happy family. . . . I had two sister-in-laws who are of different nationality, but except that my mother has difficulty in talking to them on account of language, that had made no difference." While her parents lived below them, there was close contact with the extended family. Her relationships with the community had been rather tenuous. Her feelings about her retarded child, her pride in the face of this problem were factors:

"With neighbors, I don't even now talk about it. After my visits to Southbury, if I am asked, 'How is he?' I just say 'He is fine.' That closes the conversation. To friends, family, neighbors too I say, 'Jerry is just like always.' And that is the end of it. . . . We never discussed him in the manner of speaking that it would be conversation. I'd say, 'He's like he was.' They'd ask if he was sitting, and I would say no. The older women, my mother's old friends, ask about him at church. They would say, 'Such a pity, such a pity! Such a nice family and it should happen to them!' I'd say, 'God's will.' And they would say, 'Isn't it wonderful—she takes it so beautiful!' You can't cry about it, that's about all. Even if you say that you feel bad, they can't do anything. (I never admit to anyone when I'm sick.)"

While the little boy was at home, she had enjoyed the visits of the social worker from Hartford:

"Somehow conversation with ordinary people was hard, We would talk and talk, and there would be no ending, and then I would feel so much better after talking with her—the air was clear. . . . It was after Jerry had gone that there was such a loss. I would be here alone all day long. I would think I heard him bang his head against the crib. I had to get out and meet people, hear conversation; by listening to somebody else's troubles, I forgot a little of my own."

At the time of the interview, three years after her son's admission she was still working and evidently enjoyed her three-to-eleven shift at the factory. Also, with her husband and through her girls at school, she had made a tentative venture into the community. But it was tentative: "I never had time for neighbors. This cup of coffee business with three children, I couldn't do."

She emphasized that as far as her family was concerned this problem had no effect whatsoever: "No stumbling block in any way to separate us. Nor did it bring us closer. We get along peaceably. We are not a very close family. With us everything is on the formal side." However, there was nostalgia in her recollection:

"We used to have quite a circle of friends before the children were born. It is impossible to say that it was all Jerry's being here though. We couldn't go because of Jerry. We thought, 'Why doesn't somebody come over?' The people have cars. We don't have a car. Often on Sunday we will sit here alone today and say, 'Why doesn't somebody come to see us?' We haven't gotten back in the swing of it. I do get out a little bit more with my husband now. . . .

"There's not much socially in the family except a christening. They have had a lot of them. My brothers have large families. . . . It did make a change, but we can't trace it entirely to him. Maybe it was the increase in the families. Remember how we used to have fun here and there. Part of the reason may be everybody had plans to do with their lives. Time was moving on.

"I had never gone to clubs, even before. My husband is in a private club, a fraternal organization. He used to be spare bartender at times. Now he is a director there. . . . For me all that was out, when Jerry was home, but he attended the meetings. Meetings are a pretty dry business, they're always looking for committees."

The wife gave some insight into the role of religion for her in this problem:

"Even when Jerry was home, I went to seven o'clock Mass all those years. Church comes first. I think it strengthened more the religious life. We had a reason to pray more than we would have if everything went well; and we had the prayers of the Sisters and all the friends that something might be done to help him." In her own family, "It had to be that you could not get up on your feet before you missed Mass."

There had been some economic burden upon the family too in caring for their retarded son. But the wife did not want to overstress it:

"The jobs have been steady. There was no financial or family trouble. The three children when they were small were sick a lot, but that was force of habit. There was always a medicine bottle on the refrigerator. . . .

"There was medical expense, not only from going to the different doctors, but he would get those temperatures and we would call the pediatrician. Usually when the doctor came for one, he would prescribe for all. We would have the doctor two or three times a week. When the doctor came, it was cash on the line, the same with the drugstore.

"We didn't buy anything we couldn't afford. . . . We didn't buy a car because of the house. My father didn't believe in living on a rent for young people. . . . Nothing as far as expense is concerned, we were never deprived of anything—just the social opportunities and having children in. My husband has been a hard worker all his life. In spite of his lack of training and education he has done very well. Now he is teaching others to do the work he has mastered."

The road toward commitment has been described already. The period of waiting for a place at Southbury was one of sorrow:

"The only thing we thought of—it was very hard to think of giving him up. We always looked forward to the day when he would go, so that we would have more freedom, and yet we didn't want him to go—'I hope they don't take him.' . . . You feel more for those children than you do for the healthy ones; they have never had a chance. It isn't easily forgotten. With a normal child, if something happens, you feel the grief but are able to get over it sooner. With a child like that, you cannot forget. . . .

"I figured six months to a year at the longest. We never discussed it with anybody. I didn't anticipate the long wait we had. It was nearly four years. The social worker would come with glowing reports: 'He is on the critical list. We are building a new building.' It was always the same story that she gave us. It gave me a chance to speak my piece. Here is an impersonal contact with somebody who will listen while I talk, I thought. Keeping everything in is not good. It's hard when you can't talk to somebody. Keeping this thing to yourself like that all the time, it is hard."

The process of commitment itself was uneventful. The doctors and the social worker had helped the mother prepare. She was reconciled: "There was nothing that could be done for him. After a while, it really didn't matter so much, the goals you had for him." In recalling the pangs of separation from her child she said:

"No, I do not believe it was right then and there. As the days went on, then the feeling came that we had given him up. It was like a vacuum —the next day when I took the crib apart and put it away. You're used to bumping into things and then there's this wide open space. I would always go in to look at him before I went to bed, the last thing. I still do that with the other children because I had that habit. And after he was gone, I would say to Jessica, 'Eat, and then I'll feed Little Brother.' "

While waiting to visit, the days were very long:

"It seemed the time would never come when we could see him. I used to dream of his being maltreated during the night; that he was bleeding, or fallen out of the crib. I had no fear for the care; it was the void, and missing him so much, perhaps that was the reason, and the anxiety for him."

Happily, the social worker's prior reassurances were borne out by the wife's own experience:

"From the very first visits our minds were at peace, that everything was in order as it should be and that we had nothing to fear. After my first visit when I saw what good care, I no longer had dreams. It was the week before Christmas, and it was decorated as a home would be. We felt very good when we saw how well he looked, how well taken care of. . . . They had nurses there. They did take care of them. The place was clean. With normal curiosity, I took all his clothes off and there wasn't a mark on his body. When they told me what he was fed, meat twice a day and ice cream and the methods of feeding him I felt very good, that I hadn't made a mistake in sending him. . . .

"I think they do the best they can for him. He is being put on that heated floor with the mats on it now, where they can get more exercise than in a crib. While they are in that room, there is an attendant; they are not left alone. They have music. They take turns to roll around on the floor. . . . They seem to lavish attention. They must observe those children because they tell what he does when you aren't there. They must observe each child as an individual, or else they wouldn't have that information to give me when I come. . . . What they tell me is the biggest part of what I remembered he'd do at home."

The wife justified her regular visits:

"He is still a part of our family even though he is up there. I think he requires more thought than a normal child would. It is not his fault that he is there. If his parents forget him, who will think about him?"

Her feeling of deprivation had not continued:

"No, there is no feeling at all. There's thought that he's there, but there is not that loss. I suppose time is what does it. When you know he is secure up there, you get used to it not having him home. You think about it; you know that you have him there, but that it is good for him and that you did the best you can."